*   *

*

SPECIAL DELIVERY
A PACKET OF REPLIES

*

*   *

SPECIAL DELIVERY

A PACKET OF REPLIES

BY

BRANCH CABELL

* *

*

"Heaven send thee a good delivery!"

*

WILDSIDE PRESS

Published by
Wildside Press, LLC
P.O. Box 301
Holicong, PA 18928-0301 USA
www.wildsidepress.com

Wildside Press Edition: MMIII

For
GEORGE T. KEATING

Good and evil, blending,—
Everywhere men say,—
Obscurely work at sending
Rewards on Judgment Day.

Good and evil, blending,—
Everywhere men say,—
Take no thought of ending,
Keep no ordered way,—
Eternally at play,
Aim but at interplaying. . .

Thirdly, some offend
Ineffably by saying,
Not without shrugs, *My friend,*
Good and evil blend.

CONTENTS

* *

*

*   *

*

The reader is asked to believe that all the correspondents addressed in this book are imaginary persons. Should the reader not comply with this moderate and civil request, the author must decline to accept any responsibility for such stubbornness.

*

*   *

*   *

*

THE EPISTLE
EXPLICATIVE

*

*   *

"What's this *ducdame*? 'Tis a Greek invocation, to call fools into a circle."

THE EPISTLE EXPLICATIVE

＊　　＊

＊

 $\mathcal{T}$ o you, friend, who now consider reading this book, I would explain its nature. Hereinafter I attempt to catch up with some part of my correspondence, by answering sundry letters which every male author now alive is very often called on to answer. And, while I was about it, I have written each one of these answers in two forms, the first presented form being in each case a revision of the second-given form, and an instance of my advance, in some degree, toward the great epistolary grace of brevity.

So it was the revised form I posted. Yet I have preserved the original form of each answer too, in chief because I desired to prove to you what striking changes may burgeon from a little judicious rewriting, and in part because the original version still appears to me, upon the whole, the more frank and the more self-expressive. Though brevity be a virtue, yet is truth not always a vice.

Many of my confrères, I grant, now that I come to put together this collection of replies, would have expressed themselves differently here and there, adventuring more fearlessly in the uncivil. My nature is peace-loving, it is even pigeon-livered, and must dree its weird. The point, at all events, is that, in optional forms, I have hereinafter answered ten letters which every literary man in a fair line of practice receives over and yet over again, and does not ever answer with any commensurate fullness or candor, because—it is a little-known circumstance, which I reveal, I imagine, for the first time to those millions of persons who habitually write to authors—an author's main business in life is other than to reply to unsolicited letters from strangers.

An author, it follows, does not answer these letters, as a rule, or, at most, he answers them impatiently, briefly, without thoroughness. He neglects here the obligations of civility; and for this precise reason do I revert hereinafter to the already handled topic of an author's correspondence. Of the irrational letters which every living

The Epistle Explicative

writer receives I have spoken in another place: in this place I complete my consideration of the same topic, by presenting those answers which, to my finding, the molested author ought in due courtesy to send back.

The ten letters I have answered were selected, from among some thirty competent types, as being the ten letters by which every male writer, I believe, is pestered most often. Yet it seems to me, on deliberation, that the eighth letter (which I at least receive weekly) may be less widely representative than are its comrades. Other novelists, being more lucid fellows, may be called on not quite so frequently to explain what during the progress of composition they imagined they were writing about. I, who am not omniscient, may not speak here for my confrères: but I do know that my own readers take rather a high hand with me as to this point, incessantly.

I know also that every writer of books is annoyed by schoolchildren and by reviewers, about equally, and by the young man who plans himself "to become a writer," and by that yet other ubiquitous correspondent who desires a prescribed course of reading. I know that every writer is harried by the compilers of "symposiums," and by the inscription seekers who collect "first editions," and by yet other writers who send him their books. I know that, without consulting his preferences, divers women pop out of his past, just as relentlessly as yet other women prepare to enter his future. These ills may no writer escape, so long as to write letters remains a human foible and no sane restrictions are put upon the sale of postage stamps. With these ills I deal hereinafter.

*   *

*

I would tell you also, friend and staunch patron, who have read thus far, that through considerations of space alone, in the old dignified phrase, have I been prevented from making full replies to yet other correspondents. Concerning some of these I have spoken earlier, in another place, but I elect to believe that my repetitiousness in listing all these fond nuisances yet again, in this place, is not inappropriate to the repetitiousness with which they themselves molest authors. In any case, no merely human author could well ignore at this special point:—

(Types 11-16) The person who collects autographs or book plates; the person who is (or who will be, on such-and-such a date) in Richmond and intends to call on me; the person who wishes to know the proper pronunciation of my surname or of the word "Poictesme"; the person who desires information as to his or her Virginian ancestry; the person who wants an autographed picture; and the person who seeks permission to dramatize one or another of my writings.

(Types 17-20) The young person who has just completed a literary masterpiece which he wishes me to read and have published; the young person with irregular sexual tastes who wishes to arrange a meeting; the young person who forwards a batch of manuscripts for criticism; and the young person who is writing a thesis about me for his or her graduating paper at college.

(Types 21-22) The rare book dealer who desires a letter relative to one or another book by me (to be pasted in and sold with the book); and the charitable organization, or school or college library, which asks for a donation of autographed books.

(Types 23-30) The woman who either wishes me to lecture before the local woman's club or else to furnish the material for a club paper which she is to prepare concerning me not later than next Thursday; the woman whose husband does not understand her nature; the woman who is accomplished in perverse delights (which she flavors, as a rule, with black magic); the woman who will be in Richmond overnight at the home of a friend who can be trusted; the woman who can explain what she wants to see me about only in private talk; the woman who has known me in a previous life (under the Pharaohs, usually); the woman who for no given reason writes me an intimate account of her copulations; and the young woman who wishes me to advise her whether she would do well to retain her virginity until marriage.

Now that I think about this last type, by the way, young men write almost as often to ask the same advice about their own continence: and I wonder then what the race is coming to, in the light of my memories. Nor can I understand why I should be thought to have any least interest or authority in this matter.

To each of these thirty types (with all their subdivisions, variants, fusions, and offshoots) I owe a large number of responsive letters, which just at present I have not the time to write. I reply instead to the first ten types enumerated, as being the ten correspondents by whom every male author is beset most frequently, in so far as goes my own experience.

And I deal, too, with their demands as courteously as may be. I have tried to combine the virtue of candor with an ever-present charitable remembrance that no one of these persons at bottom means to be annoying. Not through intention do they become pests, but through repetition. And repetition, I reflect meekly, is a foible which has been imputed to me also, by exceedingly well-thought-of persons very nearly as intelligent as these correspondents. It behooves me, perhaps, to condone repetition.

Even so, I admit that when I have received any letter twenty times, and have answered it twenty times, the progression begins indefinably to lack zest; with the arrival of that letter's hundredth copy I regard it, I am afraid, with active distaste: and I know that when any arithmetically mature author regards his correspondence as a whole, then the brain reels.

He perceives that for, let us say, some thirty years, thousands of persons have been writing him identical letters; and he gets an odd feeling of being lost among unhuman automatons. It does not seem to him quite possible that high heaven's handiwork in its most ambitious product should be shaped as precisely to one common model as is the output of Mr. Henry Ford.

*   *

*

Friend, do you not mistake me! I have spoken thus far of the sad average and of the leaden rule of dull-minded persons. Yet here as elsewhere the rule is proved by its exceptions; and in this instance very delightfully. For I grant, and none gladlier grants, that every once in a while the harried writer finds on his desk an unhackneyed letter from some person unknown to him, a letter both sane and appreciative, a letter which is no one of those thirty letters that the postman brings in over and over and yet over again. How then does the man's heart rejoice, leaping in its joy, with warmed cockles! and how unhappy the lark, how unpleased Punch, how little merry the grig, must seem when these are compared with that author in his bright Elysium! His sole *amari aliquid* is then tiny: he lacks a tail to wag in his doglike gratitude, but of other needs he has none.

Should this letter speak of his genius and commend his writings, such dicta will, I admit, not quell his delight; and yet praise is no necessary ingredient. What matters is to have been understood, to find that your printed book has been truly communicative, to learn that at least one person has educed from your book exactly what was put into it. Should this person not admire his eduction, he has none the less endeared himself, and he stays privileged in his howsoever imperfect taste, by his perspicacity.

This especial sort of appreciation comes to an author far more often through the kindness of his correspondents, I am afraid, than through the shears of his clipping bureau. At least one author who is well known to me regrets the restrained education of most reviewers, as a schooling which has taught them to write but not to read. It is this deficiency, he believes, which compels so many of them to invent the nature and the contents of the book they are criticizing. Of the truth of this theory I am not wholly certain: but I encounter in my scrapbooks a great many reviews which lend color to it.

Appreciation, I repeat, an author appreciates; and he finds it rarely. Into each book goes too much of his life to make indiscriminate applause and large royalties seem a fair dividend on his investments, this cormorant reflects in his insatiation. For myself, I doubt if any writer, since he already has the most happy of mortal lots, can deserve appreciation to boot: I quote only, repeating but my tribe's esurient demandings. I add that when this appreciation does come to him the postman must necessarily be its deliverer, and that such letters are an author's main reward, and indeed are his sole reward, by any magnanimous standard.

The Epistle Explicative

Such letters he answers with a proud heart, believing (in the man's really incurable folly) that his existence has been justified. To yet other letters, reduplicative and incessant, multitudinous, swarming like gnats—to letters even as are the sand grains on the seashore, and as indistinguishable the one from another—to letters ever mounting, through infernal magic, in self-propagating and many-colored heaps—to letters how far more numerous than are nowadays the hairs of his devoted head—to letters and to letters, and to yet other letters, he replies at first with tired curses, then with a curt typewritten formula, and last of all with this book.

THE FIRST LETTER

*   *

*

RUTH UNIVERSAL

My dear Child:

It was wholly a pleasure to receive your letter, and I regret that I have not time to answer it in full. Should you, however, write to my publishers, Messrs. Robert M. McBride & Company, 4 West Sixteenth Street, New York City, they will supply you with the material you need.

I hope that you may like my books,-- and I stay

Yours faithfully,

Branch Cabell

31 September 1932

RUTH UNIVERSAL

*   *

*

Your letter informs me that your class in English is studying modern authors; and, through a sequence not wholly apparent, is offering a prize for the best scrapbook. You would therefore, upon the ground that you have heard my stories are very interesting, consider it a great favor if I should send you full information concerning myself, my books, and what you comprehensively indicate as "incidents in my life," along with my picture, my book plate, and my signature. You believe that if I help you in this way you will be certain to win the prize. Your name is Ruth; you are thirteen years old; you write upon robin's egg blue paper with gilt edges; and you are a member of the Sophomore Class in an Indianian high school.

Special Delivery

Along with your letter, as it happens, I have also a letter from Millicent, who is a Junior in a Californian high school. In order to pass her English course Millicent has to complete a project (whatever that may mean) pertaining to my books. She directs me to help her by telling as much as I have time to write in a letter, which, she stipulates, must be signed by me personally, about myself, my life, my publishings, and what authors have most influenced me, "sending all material along that line," and any pictures of my home and of me which would aid Millicent in illustrating her scrapbook. "She directs," I say: for Millicent's tone is void of shilly-shallying: I imagine she is related to the county tax collector, or perhaps to the sheriff, and has observed fondly the epistolary manner of her kinsman.

Well, and yesterday I had a similar letter from Jerome, who attends a high school on Long Island; the day before yesterday I received virtually the same letter from Edward, who is in his second year at high school in Chicago; and to-morrow and the day after to-morrow, even until next May, I shall find in my morning's mail just such letters from yet other school-children.

My dear Ruth, you and your compeers have thus become an infernal nuisance. It would in some aspects be pleasant enough to devote the remainder of my life on earth to compiling amply illustrated monographs about myself, for you and Millicent and Jerome and Edward and all the others; but second thought suggests that such daily employment would hardly prove self-supporting. I am thus urged to refuse you by common-sense: to the other side, I am not able, with any comfort, to deny the request of a child, howsoever inordinate.

So I am sending you my book plate, and a photograph which I regret to say is a faithful likeness, and a long list of the books I have published, and a charitably brief pamphlet that will tell you quite enough about these books to forestall any need of your trying to read them.

But you ask also that I tell you about the author of these books. You have thus set for me a theme concerning which my views are both biased and limited through the merciful dictates of human vanity. Yet I willingly record for you, rash child, the thoughts which occur to me when I think frankly about myself.

*   *

*

I once delighted in the romances of William Harrison Ainsworth, particularly in *Crichton*. I remember when cows went at their own free will about the streets of Richmond, which city has now an estimated population of 182,929 human beings, in addition to Ellen Glasgow and John Powell and myself. Once in a while I wonder who wrote the three children's books about Tim Pippin (the giant-killer, the beloved of Princess Primrose), and if these books are still procurable anywhere? I am fond of mushrooms prepared in any fashion, but I find them least appetizing when cooked with a cream sauce. When I buy a pair of garters (of the double-grip variety) and the salesman asks me what color I prefer, I cannot imagine what dif·

ference the color of his garters can make to any man.

During the World War I served my country by designing the coat-of-arms of the Eightieth Division. I have never played golf or indulged in any form of outdoor exercise. My knowledge of butterflies is confined to the fact that the white ones feed upon cabbage leaves and the purple ones upon clover. I have not carried or pawned a watch now for some fifteen years. Of every parcel which comes to me I preserve the string and the wrapping paper with demented thrift. Such are the thoughts which occur to me when I think frankly about myself.

My blood pressure, my pulse, and my metabolism are all so abnormally low as to interest the medical profession: of the three I can understand only what my pulse is. The people of whom I am fondest appear to me to be uncommonly tedious in their talk. Although credited with murder, I was not really the philanthropist who committed it. I once renewed a subscription to *Vanity Fair*. I do not easily digest milk or ham or fried food of any sort. I have not yet

read *Ulysses*, and at this late day I in all likeli-
hood shall not ever read *Ulysses*. My birthplace
is now an upstairs room in the Richmond Public
Library.

I peculiarly enjoy the operas of Gilbert and
Sullivan, almost any compilation of folk-lore,
the odes of Horace, and William Winter's un-
intentionally comic two volumes about Richard
Mansfield. I think too much about books: it is
perhaps some retro-active effect of starting life
in what afterward became a library. I never
argue any matter with anyone except when
peach ice cream or chipped beef is served to me
in my own home. I like sunsets, genealogy,
Benedictine, illiterate women, and small china
animals. With my dinner coat I continue to
wear a turn-down collar. Such are the thoughts
which occur to me when I think frankly about
myself.

I do virtually all my own typewriting, em-
ploying only the forefinger of each hand, and
the left forefinger but for the shift keys. In
dressing I am careful every morning to put on
the right foot sock first. In addition to the books
I have published I wish that I had also written,

with a deal of compression, *Le Vicomte de Bragelonne*, and *Henry Esmond* very much as it stands. I can never think of anything to say to a clergyman. Thunderstorms frighten me. I understand nothing whatever about motor cars except that it is a point of honor to go up all hills in high, and that the radiator is the thing in front.

It does not seem logical that I have looked at every painting and sketch and water color in the Musée Gustave Moreau (including the three hundred little ones in the revolving stand), but have not yet seen Niagara Falls. To touch the skin of a peach sets my teeth on edge: so does the sight of a cut and wilted flower. I am stingy in small money matters. I dislike nobody, now that Woodrow Wilson is dead. In writing prose I observe that I do not naturally employ the *Ionic a minore* or the third pæon. I support twenty-eight goldfish, each of whom has his or her own name. I have never been cordially moved by philanthropy or altruism. When a dentist is working on my teeth I find it an immense comfort to wave both feet in the air.

Such are the thoughts which occur to me when I think frankly about myself.

Into the drift of new days I forbear to pry after dreams as large and ardent as those which swayed my far-away youth-time. Then I had grief, love, and laughter: now I am fairly contented. Life, which was tragic or blissful, becomes a more moderate commerce. All that is done seems well done with; all that I keep well contents me; all that awaits I must meet, God willing, without any whining. So much alone one may gain from the half of a century's schooling—platitudes flavored with gratitude. That is life's stinted tuition's end, in so far as I fathom it. Such are the thoughts which occur to me when I (who attempt this rarely) think frankly about myself.

*   *

*

I have set down these particulars as they occur to me, my dear Ruth, so that you may duly communicate them to the teacher who suggested that you write the letter which I now answer. In addition, I am asking you to tell your teacher that, apart from the present good standing of the *monologue intérieur*, I have yet further literary authority for answering a fool (by which I do not at all mean you, my dear) according to his folly. I would like you also to inform your teacher that I esteem him (or, it may be, her) as a most meritorious candidate for the cucking stool, the knout, the bastinado, and the decisive torture of the Pilliwinckes.

For while one does not look for distinguished mental ability within the confines of a high school, I do think that even a school teacher is none the worse off for an occasional gleam of intelligence and common-sense. Yet week after week these jacks-in-office, to every appearance, are inciting their pupils to read my books—in itself a venial and even a generous idiocy—and to write me such letters as I have indicated. I assert here no pre-eminence in affliction: every author known to me is annoyed over and yet over again with such letters. Authors have come to regard such letters as an unavoidable custom, as a sort of nuisance tax upon the second edition.

Special Delivery

From every high school in the country, I infer, scores upon scores of such letters are sent out every week during the school term. And as a rule some sort of prize is offered for the child who secures the most comprehensive and most lively extortion from his or her auctorial victim. The entire process has, in brief, become a custom.

It follows that of all the pests who annoy me with the connivance of the United States Post Office Department, you, my dear Ruth, are the most pestiferous. The others can at worst be ignored with a clean conscience: but one views a child rather differently. A child of thirteen, if there were nothing else, is just about to begin a life sentence in the penitentiary of mature existence; and one really does prefer in these last moments to gratify the least wishes of the condemned. Your scrapbook, and your English course, and the prize which you may or may not win, will very soon not matter to you, I know: but the point is that they do matter now. Everything matters at thirteen. It is indeed the beginning of a time of life so full of emotion and breathlessness and surprise, and so brief, that (as

I but now suggested) you ought to waste no moment of this not wholly happy but wholly interesting season upon books.

*   *

*

In fact I am here tempted to advise you throughout the length of your mortal living to avoid
books consistently. Books have their merits, such
merits as old Richard De Bury has well expressed
in a fine medley of Scriptural metaphors. Books,
let us grant with him, are golden urns in which
manna is laid up, they are rocks flowing with
honeycombs; they resemble the four-streamed
river of Paradise, whereby the human mind is
fed, and the arid intellect is moistened and wa-
tered; they are even as fruitful olives, as vines of
Engaddi, and as fig-trees knowing no sterility.
But I incline to part company with the bibli-
ophilic Bishop of Durham when he adds that
books are burning lamps to be ever held in the
hand.

Yet I don't know: no sane person lights a lamp

before dusk, and toward the evening of life it is true that books do come in well enough to kill time for a stinted while before time kills you. The figure holds, it may be, barring only the word "ever"; for one should remember, if but tacitly, that books can afford at best a stopgap between the serious doings of any well-conditioned life. Books, in brief, have been vastly over-advertised.

The self-evident trouble here is that all the millions of imposing pæans written and printed about books have originated perforce among writers. Indeed I myself have composed several of them. It is well therefore to appraise these sayings in somewhat the same spirit which one extends to the no less eloquent encomia of shaving creams and of ginger ales and of toothpastes encountered in the back of most magazines: the sentiments expressed there are lofty, and altruistic, and for the while convincing; yet they have been prepared, after all, by the proprietors of these delights, with a noble design to make of these supreme human blessings merchandise.

Just so, most of the fine things which writers have said about books, and about literature in general, do come to us as a sort of glorified "sales talk." Books, as one should say, are well enough in their proper place: but during your youth at any rate, my dear Ruth, that place is, I rather think, on the bookshelf.

There are, you see, when a girl is young, so very many other things to do except to read with the light falling properly at your left shoulder, things which will not hold over and await meekly a deferred engagement, as will Dante and Shakespeare, or marriage and death. I shall not indicate these things beyond the safe statement that most of them require the avoidance of any serious sequel and the co-operancy of a boy. Yet it does occur to me in this place that I was once privileged to hear Mr. Joseph Hergesheimer address a girls' school. He exhorted his enthralled young hearers very movingly, I remember, to pay no further attention whatever to their assigned studies, nor to the possible comments of their teachers, but to remember always that the main duty of every girl was to acquire charm, since charm was the sole needed asset of womanhood. I incline to agree with Mr. Hergesheimer, in so far that I think a woman who possesses the indefinable quality called charm need lack for nothing else in a worldful of men all eager, and many of them able, to satisfy her desires. She has but (in the words of yet another competent instructor of young women) to be good to some man who can be good to her, and all bright blessings will be added to her abundance.

To the other side, I do reflect that one may not properly nurture that which one lacks. I do not believe that feminine charm is a matter to be acquired by painstaking, like the French language or a bank account, but think it to be an innate gift highly cultivable. And to my finding not one woman child in a hundred—but what do I say! not one, I mean, in a thousand—is born with that same indefinable quality called charm. To those luckless women who compose the unmagnetic majority, books, I admit, can do no great hurt: books properly selected may even help them by-and-by to become physicians or social workers or United States senators or very famous novelists, and may in this way mitigate by not a little their predestined failure in life.

But upon this matter, my dear child, I am

prejudiced. I know only that the woman whom I find most attractive, and by far the most inexplicably contented, avoids books somewhat as I myself avoid watermelons, not out of any active distaste but simply as one who finds them not worth bothering with. In fact, during our twenty years' acquaintanceship she has to my knowledge read but two books from beginning to end, these peculiarly favored volumes being Mr. Bernard Shaw's *Love Among the Artists* and Mr. Sinclair Lewis's *Free Air*. My own books she has looked into, as each first came from the publishers, and has then put aside without comment—and yet too with the sort of silence which made me feel I was getting off rather lightly.

But that is hardly the point. The real point is that I envy this marvelously gifted woman's capacity to meet author after author, and to get on with them handsomely (even be they female) without affecting the least interest in, or the most faint notion of ever reading, their balderdash. It is a truly breath-taking accomplishment which I, who am made of feebler stuff, can but covet hopelessly. I reflect perforce what a vast deal of double-dealing and what tedious sessions of time-wasting this accomplishment, if but I possessed it, would save me, day after day, when I meet precisely the same authors. And it is an accomplishment, too, which keeps me in a meek state of unwillingness to believe that any woman child, in a world wherein almost anybody is rather more than apt to be married occasionally by an author, can be well prepared against her future through enforced contact with books. I incline contrariwise, after thus confessing my unavoidable bias, to resent this notion.

Above all do I resent the notion that my books, of all books, should be inflicted upon an undefended girl child, along with algebra and geography and spelling and yet other nuisances of school life. I wish very heartily, my dear Ruth, that you could understand the unimportance and the evanescence of all these matters. As a cloud passes, so will they depart from you imperceptibly.

You will never note their going. Only by-and-by in the unerudite hours of maturity, when nobody who is worth knowing knows anything in particular, will you recall that dark tyranny of useful and improving knowledge which molested your girlhood contemporaneously with mumps and chicken pox and pimples. From every one of these youthful ills—at fifty-three, let us say—you will have recovered forever: they will then seem to you as dim and futile as at that date will seem the first gawky boy to take liberties with your person: you will recall these matters, if at all, with the same vague smiling. Geography and algebra and that man in Virginia's books, whoever he was, will be at one with pimples and the finger-nail which hurt you a little very long ago: none will matter a bean's worth to the slack hedonism of your middle age.

*   *

*

I know that for my part, when I reflect on my own Merovingian school days, and upon the many things which I was then taught, and which I once "knew," I am divided between self-admiration and a wonder which, within reasonable limits, is wild with all regret. And it seems to me a sound parable.

For I admire, I repeat, without in the least bit envying, my erstwhile accomplishments. With all history how familiar was I (fond memory now remarks, in a state of proper pride), with what lists of monarchs at my finger-tips, and with leading dates and decisive battles at the tip of my tongue! What countries could I not bound, with a crisp résumé of the capital of each, the larger cities, main rivers, and chief exports, in the same hour that I dealt masterfully with compound interest and cube roots and cosines? In many languages was I skilled. I harbored information as to irregular French verbs, and I knew the approved order of adverbial clauses under varying conditions in Germany; I discovered for myself that the dullness of *Don Quixote* had not been inserted by the Anglophobe who translated this dreadful book into English; I was very learned in the metres of Catullus and Horace, and I wrote with my own hands a monograph upon the verbals in *-tos* as they are employed by Æschylus. It is really wonderful how much I have forgotten. There was calculus, for instance: I graduated in this science with full honors; but to-day, beyond a prevailing impression that some of it was differential, and that you did it on a large blackboard and so got your finger-nails uncomfortably full of chalk, I have no least notion as to what calculus was like.

Well, but my point is that to-day the history has all been rewritten and the geography thoroughly changed (with a neat filling up, I observe, of the interior of Africa and the two polar regions) so that the most of what I once knew as to these matters is to-day not true, even if I could remember any of it. What was taught me as to astronomy and psychology appears to-day as unveracious as what was taught me about the prevalence of Anglo-Saxon influence in the higher reaches of our racial character and literature. It develops that (after the long years I gave over to revering them) there were no Anglo-Saxons. Their vacated eminence in learned esteem has been filled by Nordics. The chemistry I studied in the basements of William and Mary might as well have been acquired from Paracelsus at the University of Basel. Hardly a word of it holds true any longer. Even physics,

they tell me, does not adhere to its former views
of lightning rods and crystallization and the infallibility of Sir Isaac Newton: so that here too
I did but laboriously amass a great deal of mis-
information. Only a little of that which I learned
about literature, in brief, remains unshaken, and
yet clings to me as a ruthless impediment to my
ever winning a Pulitzer prize or to my being
taken in, in any sense, by the National Institute
of Arts and Letters.

*   *

*

I have not a doubt, my dear Ruth, that a majority of the things you are now being taught at
your Indianian school (including the advisability
of a polite interest in my books) will, by the
time when you have happily forgotten all about
these tedious matters, be equally discredited.
You may perceive then, in due season, that these
impositions of your school days (*quorum pars
fui*, without in the least intending it) are in some
sort a parable. All through our lives the teacher,

in one or another high disguise, stands at our elbows, eternally teaching, and for the most part teaching nonsense. Yet the name of every well-thought-of teacher, under all robings and honorary degrees, is custom; and we must all listen respectfully, because custom teaches at each particular moment the approved sum of human wisdom.

By-and-by perhaps one notices that the lessons are inconsistent, and deviate from what was taught yesterday: as it was taught me, for example, that the interior of Africa was for all practical purposes vacant (the reports from no exploring party led by H. Rider Haggard being considered final), just so was it then taught that Jehovah sat immediately overhead, that no virtuous woman smoked, and that mutton suet cured colds. Upon none of these four tenets does custom insist to-day: we are told of quite other eternal verities: and I for one must continue to listen to this never-resting instructor with rather more of respectfulness than of faith. For against this great and universal teacher I at fifty-three am powerless, and as inefficient as you are at thirteen to resist the dictates of that lesser dullard who has prompted you to annoy me with your absurd blue and gilt letter.

So do I approach my moral. This, Ruth, is the whole parable: we are all at school every day of our lives; and but a little of what we are taught remains true overnight. The familiar verities and all the generally accepted knowledge, nay, even the tacit assumptions and the most simple axioms, of each human generation are discarded unceasingly. They are put aside with a continuance so inflexible that every morning their revered pedestals are occupied by fresh fallacies. Indeed, the approved sum of human wisdom has been altered, somewhere, in the very while that you read this sentence; and facts which were undeniable but a heart-beat back have become no longer true.

Yet always, at every instant, custom teaches us, This and this only is the entire truth at last, this and this only is demanded of the well-thought-of person now and forever. And custom does not put up with any least scepticism in the while that custom continues to instruct the civilized in the established faith of all rational beings during this particular forenoon.

Ruth Universal

It is a situation wherein the observant pupil may well temper a respectful attitude with some inner dubiety: yet he will perform each task, meanwhile—just as you and I are doing, my dear, —which the teacher directs. To do that is neither brilliant nor heroic; but it is relatively safe. And to such truisms about life do we, in the end, return.

THE SECOND LETTER

*　　*

*

"THE BREAST OF THE NYMPH"

My dear Sir:

It was wholly a pleasure to
receive your letter, and I thank you
most cordially for the kind things
which you say concerning my work.

I regret, in all sincerity,
that it is not possible, just now,
for me to answer your various
questions. But after all there is,
to my finding, only one rule for
good writing,-- to write that which
you really desire to write, in the
way which seems best to you.

Yours faithfully,

Branch Cabell

31 September 1932

"THE BREAST OF THE NYMPH"

*   *

*

$\mathcal{Y}$*ou have written out for me, O most enviable* young fool, a list of questions which you desire me to answer as a guide for your future, so that you may "become a writer." Each question has a ring so familiar that I may not guess how often, how incredibly often, I have received your pathetically brisk, and forthright, and business-like, and moonstruck letter before I received it, yet again, to-day.

You are, you inform me (and indeed you almost always are) one of the editors of your college magazine. You are "majoring in English," and besides your pursuit of "other English courses for necessary backgrounds," you are, you tell me, the member of "a creative writing class." You have set every commended trap, in brief, to capture the straying muse in order that you may domesticate her out-of-hand as your helpmate in letters.

"Am I," you continue, in somewhat the pouncing manner of a lawyer who discredits a witness, "on the right track? Should I imitate the style of so-called model authors in my writing? If so, whom would you suggest? Should I get a few years' experience on a newspaper? I have an idea that it is well to become steeped in classicism. I am working conscientiously to that end. Is it advisable to continue? Or should I study present-day literature more?"

And yet other question upon question do you put to me, about such irrelated matters as art and Mr. Ludwig Lewisohn and magazine editors and the best book of synonyms, out of an engaging belief that I, who have no least interest in your welfare, will be willing to devote a day or so to answering all these questions one after the other.

Still, it is not difficult to answer your questions. The reply, the reply to every one of them, is that I do not know. It is my private opinion that whether you do or do not do any of the things about which you inquire will not matter a straw's weight in your possible evolution as an author. It is also my absolute conviction that whether or not you do eventually "become a writer" is an affair in which I have not the tiniest interest. In brief, I can see no logical reason why I should not drop your letter into the waste-paper basket, and so have done with both your infernal briskness and you.

Instead, I fall awondering why you should want—or at least should temporarily imagine that you want—"to become a writer"? The term, to begin with, is staggeringly vague. People write all manner of oddments, such as verse, and society columns, and sermons, and advertising copy. Yet I believe your term is apt enough. I look back, across some seven lustres, to the time when I too was the editor of a college magazine, and when I too debated most of the questions you raise, and when I too meant "to become a writer." For there was never any doubt in my mind, after my sixteenth year or thereabouts, that I would "become a writer." And yet there was never any definite notion, I am sure, what form this writing was to take. There was, most certainly, no stimulating delu-

sion that writers were rewarded with affluence
or high station.

*   *

*

Authorship was not esteemed in the Virginia of
my boyhood, and in fact, for all practical purposes, authorship was unknown there. Upon but
two flesh-and-blood writers had the eyes of my
adolescence rested; and none, in so far as I knew,
thought of these two as being, primarily, writers.
One was Amélie Rives, whose first novels were
then being read furtively in Richmond, with
shocked zest, as really not at all the sort of thing
which you might expect from an unmarried girl,
and as, in brief, books which the well-bred must
blandly ignore when such books were published
by a Rives of Albemarle,—and the other was
Thomas Nelson Page, who, in Richmond, was
esteemed and made much of on the ground that,
apart from being "one of the real Pages," he had
married considerable money in taking his second
wife.

"The Breast of the Nymph"

A bit later, to be sure, when I was at college, I heard that the youngest Glasgow girl had published a book, but by that time my business in life was fixed, nor did I remember clearly which one of the five was Ellen. It comes back to me that my informant, whom Appomattox had retired from lieutenant-colonelcy in the Confederate Army, described it as one of the most damnable things he had ever heard of in his life, that Frank Glasgow's daughter should be getting mixed up with that sort of thing. Since my informant too had a daughter, in whom my young eyes could detect no flaw nor any imperfection at that season, I have no doubt I looked respectfully sympathetic.

No, when I was your age there was no tangible prompting for me to turn author. The sin of Virginia was written with a pen of iron, and with the point of a diamond, as Jeremiah has failed to remark: it was graven upon the tombstone of her dead excellence. She had not honored any artist. She had esteemed only the cheap and ready glories of big words spoken in her praise, and in the praise of all her customs, by the equally cheap and the far, far more ready demagogue: the word which is written Virginia had not rewarded.

The leather-lunged congressmen and the braying senators she took into her bed of love, and they defiled her with loud platitudes: she doted also upon divers retired, but not at all retiring, Confederate veterans, whose voice was as the voice of asses. To the roaring of wild pastors she hearkened amorously. All these had bruised her teats so that her breasts might nurse the young no longer. With all these never-idle talkers Virginia had played the wanton in a little corner, in the plashed mire of her stagnant backwaters, saying, Speak to me of my pre-eminence! And all they had spoken to the desire of Virginia, very egregiously.

Of beauty and of chivalry and of gray legions they spoke, and of a fallen civilization such as the world will not ever see again, and, for that matter, never did see; of a first permanent settlement, and of a Mother of Presidents, and of a republic's cradle, and of Stars and Bars, and of yet many other bygones, long ago at one with dead Troy and Atlantis, they babbled likewise for interminable years, without ever, ever ceasing. The wind blew away their words as each word was spoken: still did they vocalize in the wind's teeth.

There were no written words to outlive their babblings, for Virginia did not read, nor did she honor any writer. She doted only upon the big words which the aspiring candidate bellowed, or which gray little men with chin whiskers declaimed weepingly from the platform or from the pulpit. She honored stucco idols. She honored mush. No honest writer might thrive in Virginia. There was no art of any kind in Virginia. There was but an endless braying. All these things did I behold there in the days of my youth: nor are these ills yet dulcified, to express the matter just as mildly as possible.

*   *

*

No, when I was your age, my dear sir, there was no least tangible prompting for me to write; nor did I have any notion as to what I intended to write. There was simply the blind and very strong instinct, much such as you voice now, "to become a writer."

So near as I may judge, every person who eventually does in any serious sense "become a writer" is conscious in his youth of this large dim vocation. The *poietes,* the "maker," is called by what power he knows not, to make things out of words. It is as though a spell has been laid upon him, after the approved Hellenic fashion, through one brief and chance-given sight of un-veiled beauty, revealing that which seemed not utterly human, but an ambiguous and in some degree a more sinister loveliness than men seek ordinarily. He has seen this but as a gleaming beheld only in part and only for the space of a heart-beat—a space wherein the beholder's heart did not beat at all, but faltered between terror and worship and longing. He has seen, some-how, what Swinburne, in one rare moment of lucidity, has called "the breast of the nymph in the brake." It is that matter, I think, which every true romantic tries at one time or another to commemorate in words: yet if you reply with a blank stare I can but hastily agree with your common-sense.

"The Breast of the Nymph"

Nor do I mean to speak further of this matter. For this is, I admit, a matter with which the ordered life and the slowly garnered wisdom of man's race have no concern, and of which human reason may well doubt the civic and economic worth. It is a trivial matter which the aging deny with shrugged shoulders; they speak also of hormones and of Freud, of chlorosis and of puberty, with smug noddings: but the eyes of young men have seen this matter, and they stay perturbed.

So at least I believe; and if I happen to be wrong I can always reply in self-defence that it is by no means for the first time. I believe too that in youth the elect writer envisages in some sort, very far away, the notions which are some day to be his notions. They have not yet entered his mind. But he glimpses them as remote and lovely and dear wraiths, and he knows that by-and-by they will become clear and intimate. He does not, through heaven's mercy, foreknow what tyrannous taskmasters they will prove, nor what tricksters either. He is conscious only of their allure and of a magic to which his inmost being responds. In his youth the elect writer is thus doubly a nympholept, in that his seeing is bedazzled also by the resplendent beauty which is by-and-by, he knows, to inform his books.

The question is but whether he have the strength of mind to conquer all these aberrations. It has been justly observed that many men are poets in their youth, but that nevertheless (although Rossetti phrases the outcome with a difference) the most of them get over it quite satisfactorily. They get over it, and they evolve, along with the average of mankind, into the respectable practitioners of one or another respected profession, with no nonsense about them. The routine of common-sense engulfs them: they put on flesh and develop bank accounts; in a thicket they look to find no more than a lost golf ball or a spot handy for urination. They become, in brief, mature: and the world is thus happily stocked with book buyers, who endeavor through fine literature to recapture some seeming of their lost youth.

*　　*

*

"*The Breast of the Nymph*"

With the professional creative writer who has any spark of genius the case is otherwise. He does not forget that silvery strange gleam. He retains always some immaturity, in a ratio so direct to his ultimate importance as to suggest that literary talent is but a form of arrested development. He has need of this immaturity, God knows, in his droll trade. For, as you may see a child a-gallop upon a non-existent horse, just so must the creative writer direct and restrain and spur this or the other non-existent character until all have galloped or cantered, or have limped half-foundered, it may be, to the appointed goal post of his Explicit. He does not, in fine, with the comparative temperance of Tom o' Bedlam, call for a horse of air to get him through this world, but elects to drive a lean herd of phantoms tallyho. That is his business in life: and it will not bear looking at rationally.

It follows that the elect writer is not, and cannot afford to be, in any mundane sense, rational. To the contrary, for the sake of his writings' health and gusto he must cherish an all-pervading illogic, which under cool inspection appears not far removed from feeble-mindedness. And he does. None who has been much thrown with accomplished and original writers can fail to note their peculiar childishness. Here is the child's vanity, and the unchecked impulsiveness, the unreason, the naïve lying, the petulance, the catch-as-catch-can morality of a child, displayed, as it were, all over the place.

Now as touches this point, of "temperament," the romantic writer at least has back of him some weight of rowdy tradition and his own old legend of wine and garrets shared tête-à-tête. To discover any professed romantic who did not hold any such irregular traffic regularly would be, in fact, as unsettling as to learn that your bootlegger was a total abstainer: it would cause you to deal elsewhere. Yet I do not find that to compose the most painstaking sort of "realism" tends to make its writer a bit more credible as a human being. I have known sundry "realists," and each one of them was a fine triumph of fantasy. You have but to think about Sherwood Anderson or Sinclair Lewis, for example, to perceive that either of these two authors, if put by conjuration into any one of his own books, would flaunt among the sombre creatures of his fancy like a flaming phœnix or a red-and-gold hippogriffin.

Creative writers of every kind, in brief, appear to me to be rather fantastically gifted children—like changelings who as yet remember a little magic picked up in their faëry nurseries,— and they do not ever, except in exteriors, become mature. They can play at being grown-up, of course, like all other children; and some of them can do it quite well for an hour or so. But at bottom each knows that he cannot afford the comfortable ossifications of real maturity. He knows that creative literature is but a variant of the child's game "let's pretend," and that to excel in it requires the retention of a childish turn of mind.

If I appear to belittle creative literature by pointing out that it (like many other high matters, such as religion, or a sense of honor, or the institution of marriage) makes but a poor showing in the cold light of intelligence, that is far from my design. I intend, rather, a compliment. Age and experience will teach the considerate to distrust every exercise of human intelligence, and to observe that life is made livable only through a wise choice in delusions. The artist in letters and the patrons of the artist in letters are all deluded after a most handsome and comfort-giving fashion, I think, and nobody ought to ask more.

*   *

*

But to return, my dear sir, to your brisk demands. I can say only that the creative writer needs, to begin with, and to sustain him even to the wrought-iron gates of the cemetery, a peculiar order of childish unreason which will permit, day in and day out, his following after he does not know precisely what, into regions of which he can have no foreknowledge beyond the fact that they in all probability do not exist. Such unreason is the one requisite of a successful wordmonger, and the one way to acquire it is to be born with it. In other words, *poeta nascitur*. Nor is this congenital unreason to be regarded as, of necessity, a misfortune. Sometimes, to be sure, it leads the creative writer into the traditionary rags and gutters. At other times it results in a quite comfortable livelihood, as go things physical, and the man is not nominally an outcast.

I admit that the difference here is not so great as you might think. The born poet remains always a nympholept. He remembers, even when surrounded with affluence and royalty statements, that equivocal vision which in his youth did now and then, if but for the space of a heartbeat, appear to be a vital and tangible and nearby matter. It seems to be near him no longer in middle life: it thins: it comes rarelier: and by him it remains unattained forever. He questions the truth of this matter: and yet he cannot question those stinging, half-derisive memories of this matter, which keep him, even in his luxurious town home, and in his trim country residence, and in the warm arms of enamored ladies, an outcast from the comfortable repetitions and mufflings of mature life.

He who has once heeded this matter, and who has not put it out of his mind resolutely, as

a mere delusion, can have no human intimates;
and he knows it. He is conscious of that never-
ending loneliness which more mature persons
drug with the routine of common-sense affairs.
Among the well-satisfied he hungers after he
does not clearly know what; there was but a
silvery flashing, half-seen, not wholly seen, to
awaken inexplicable desires: and he lives as the
lost heir of a kingdom of whose existence he is
by no means convinced.

Meanwhile he gives all time and labor to his
art, to that insatiable fetish which demands not
only time and labor, but requires also that its
devotee's most private emotions shall be displayed in cold print. You have read, I am sure,
during your endeavors "to become steeped in
classicism," the old myth of Atys; and you thus
know that a goddess may be served with unconscionable tribute. Well, and creative literature is
not a whit less exigent than was Cybele. All de-
cency and all reserve must the fond fanatic of
letters give over to his art, to an art which he
studies so zealously that in due course he becomes conscious of its unimportance in the continuous flowing away of time, which abducts all

things, by-and-by, even the newest and most talked about books.

*   *

*

Am I counselling you, it may be you will ask, not "to become a writer"? To counsel anybody about anything was not ever a custom with me, my dear sir. To write books has diverted me now for some thirty years; it appears to me, in my more reasonable moments, a singularly futile and childish and thankless task; and yet, for no reason ever revealed to me, I have enjoyed doing it. I am but pointing out (and proving, also, by the force of example) that the elect writer is fashioned not through any course of training but through his innate irrationality.

I must point out likewise that whatsoever follows the present stage in your career must necessarily prove an anticlimax. It is the defect of those notions which woo the elect writer in his youth, when they become apparent but have not yet entered his mind, that they do not ever sur-

render to his ardors wholly. All nymphs are thus
evasive. They do, it may be, come a bit closer
by-and-by, like unwilling models approaching
an artist in whom they have no great faith; and
to some degree each notion will consent, as it
were, to sit for its portrait with marked restive-
ness. Then, while each tarries impatiently, the
poor man does the very best he can with his ad-
jectives and his commas, and he manages to
catch, perhaps, a sort of likeness. And for the
while he takes pride in that which he has done,
not knowing his doom.

After a little, though, he notices that in some
especial bit of work he has produced no supreme masterpiece. Upon every aging artist, I
think, dawns in this way, very gradually, the
horrible and astounding doubt that his genius
may be not unparalleled in the world's history.
It is a contingency at which no elect writer need
ever glance in his youth. Nor does he.

But the aging author when he turns back to
his beloved own books—and to so infernally
many of them, too!—in which there was once no
flaw to be discovered, in which but yesterday
the sprightliest wit frolicked and so much of

beauty revelled statelily, he does rather wonder to find these books pullulating, overnight, as it were, with the inadequate and the awkward. Sentences which he had remembered as being of his unalloyed best have taken on a flavor of stale pie crust; here the rhetoric both lumbers and gushes, like a street-sprinkling wagon; and now entire paragraphs stun him with the bludgeon of his own dullness. There is, in brief, no more dreadful reading for any honest writer than he must find inevitably in his own books, after a while. Those lovely notions which so elvishly allured him into so much of heart-breaking labor are simply not apparent anywhere; they have hired him, for a life-time, with fairy gold. And they themselves, he reflects, those comely and light nymphs, they are busied at their appointed task, very far away from him now, in search of still another stripling, who is not yet ensnared, but who already plans "to become a writer."

THE THIRD LETTER

*   *

*

FOR RHADAMANTHUS, SMILING

My dear Sir:

It was wholly a pleasure to
receive your letter, and your
discriminating but friendly review
has left me your debtor doubly.
For my soul's health I shall refrain
from quite believing all the kind
things you say, but that in no way
impairs my delight in them.

I am grateful beyond words,
-- and I stay

Yours faithfully,

Branch Cabell

31 September 1932

FOR RHADAMANTHUS, SMILING

* *

*

It was kindly of you, dear master, to send your review of my book; and all which you have to say of me therein is so affable I can entertain no least doubt that upon this special occasion you suffer from the fatal virtue of meaning well. The emotion with which I address you should in consequence be gratitude: it is a sad commentary upon human nature that to the contrary I approach you in envy.

With a most despairing envy do I regard the estate of you and of all your peers who write book reviews, disposing equably of your praise and your blame to us who write mere books as your underlings. That consciousness of one's own human fallibility which preys now and then upon lesser mortals gives you a wide berth (if one may thus far understate matters) and does not rear insidiously upon Olympus its interrogative head: no uncertainty plagues you: you do not voice opinions, but judgments, in tones which may perhaps remain jocular, or even friendly, but which know not ever any taint of self-distrust. How in the world, dear master, do you manage it? How does one raise, we will say, a proper self-respect to quite that pitch and luxuriance? I have seen you and talked with you, and I so know you to be a normally conducted person in private life; and I can but wonder what afflatus descends upon and possesses you, in common with all your fellow practitioners, whensoever you set to work to dispose of your daily book?

*   *

*

Three assumptions you of your craft must perforce make: that what you have to say is of some importance, that it will be respectfully weighed by an audience of fair magnitude, and that you are superior, at least slightly superior, to the au-

For Rhadamanthus, Smiling

thor whom you have under consideration. That
last tenet, in fact, is very often true: masterpieces
do not visit your desk every day; and your con-
descensions are then justified. The difficulty, to
the one side, is that a book of such costive merits
as not to outweigh your own fugitive journalism
is rather obviously not worth the pains of reviewing; to the other side, there occur now and
again those awkward moments when your betters come up before you for judgment.

I can still recall, for example, your review of
Rudyard Kipling's last book. It was, as reviews
go, an entertaining production, urbane and clem-
ent, but decisive. You attended the funeral of a
once distinguished talent; you admitted civilly
the Victorian achievements of Mr. Kipling, not
profound work perhaps, and undoubtedly much
overrated by his generation, but still quite so-so;
and you deplored that his gifts, such as they
once were, should all have lapsed into dotage.
You were wholly convincing as to Mr. Kipling's
past, present, and future, during the ten minutes
it took to read your article, and I found myself
in a glow of cordial agreement.

At the eleventh minute it occurred to me, as a

most unfair circumstance, that Mr. Kipling's last book would be duly incorporated into his collected works, to survive there, if not as the main ornament of the collection, at least as a lasting addition; and that this book would continue to be reprinted and to be read, some while after both our demises, by a fair number of persons who will never even know that your article was written. It occurred to me, in brief, that your so nicely expressed, your judicious, and your really brilliant opinion of Mr. Kipling was for all practical intent valueless.

You were dealing, through no fault of your own, with your superior; you were not, and even to-day are not, dear master, Mr. Kipling's equal, by any imaginable standards. You were passing judgment where your jurisdiction happened not to hold, somewhat as if the National Council of Monaco were to vote an amendment to the Constitution of the United States. Meanwhile the necessity put upon you by the requirements of your trade, during these irrelevant formalities, to patronize and to correct Mr. Kipling, did for the time display you in a light so uncaptivating that I am sure we can all rejoice it was but a will-o'-the-wisp glitter, gone forever within the same moment it was apparent, when the esteemed journal to which you contribute was laid aside.

In very much the same way did you dispose of Bernard Shaw's last publication, and (for very much the same reasons) here again did you suggest that your taste and your judgment, and your common-sense even, are allowed a vacation whensoever you deal with a major figure in current letters. It is perhaps as well: for in all such instances you face an *impasse*. Just as Shakespeare is not to be deduced in his great entity from *King Lear* alone, or from *Twelfth Night* alone, or from *Titus Andronicus* alone, equally is it impossible for any writer with a career so long, so various, and so glittering as is the career of Mr. Shaw, to be judged by any one of his productions; and that is the sole criterion allowed to them of your craft. Mr. Shaw, I would put it, has erected during the last forty years a secure edifice: and you attempted, you attempted perforce, to appraise its architecture by discussing one of the bricks used in this building.

You could but add to the droll falsity of your

position by condescending to Mr. Shaw during the process, and this you did with a large gusto. Your comedy was of the first order. You were not, as your readers quite understood, the equal of Mr. Shaw, by any imaginable standards: but you could play, with a well-practised art, that you were immeasurably his superior. So you entertained us all by dispensing patronage and grave gibes and aggrieved headshakings where you owed deference; and by making in every other respect a delightfully solemn ass of yourself, dear master, after the very best tradition and the immemorial privilege of your trade whensoever you encounter genius.

It must be to you, I imagine, a sound and unfailing comfort that we few persons who read your articles can get through any one of them within ten minutes, once and for all: thereafter the crumpled paper you adorn goes to the waste basket, en route to the Salvation Army wagon, and nobody thinks any more about your morning's masterpiece. You are thus made immune to that bugbear of little minds which is called consistency. It is a position I desiderate. But my deeper envy is reserved for the entrancement in

which you labor; for some of those masterly articles which delight and edify us for ten minutes
may take even longer to compose; and to imagine
oneself the superior of Bernard Shaw or of
Rudyard Kipling for a whole quarter of an hour
should be to any hack writer a delusion exhilarat-
ing enough to brighten the entire day.

And that, dear master, is but a beginning.
There is no bound to your multitudinary and
endless pleasures. From a new book by Mr.
Hergesheimer or by Mr. Sinclair Lewis, or by
Ellen Glasgow or Edith Wharton, or by any
other writer of praiseworthy achievements, you
extract the same hurtless delight in the while
that you play at being more important than some
one of these really important persons. You do
not, I suppose, imagine in uninspired hours that
your position in letters compares favorably with
the position of, let us say, Ellen Glasgow. You
must know, in your milder moments, that it behooves any living reviewer to approach Ellen
Glasgow with obeisances. Yet, when once the
afflatus of reviewing informs you, and so long as
you are appraising any book by Ellen Glasgow,

you can patronize and reprove, and put her to rights generally, without the least qualm.

It does not seem droll to you, not then, that you should instruct a genius such as you do not possess how to practise an art in which you do not pretend to competence. For I think you are quite honest about it. There appears to be in the mere physical act of writing a review something which begets a fine kindling of self-confidence and a deific state of mind such as less privileged persons induce with alcohol. There is no writer but must envy all them of your craft, who partake of this supernal pleasure at will.

For the inexperienced, the young, and the ignorant, the divine brew of reviewing is a tipple too heady. It follows that upon the nominally literary page of the local Sunday paper in many lesser cities one may find the "cub reporters," those helots of journalism, exhibited, after the old Spartan fashion, very much in their cups, as they babble there in befuddled gravity as to the month's new books. They know, these unfortunate young, they well know in their sober moments, that upon no subject beneath the sun is

78

their opinion of any value: it is their calling instead to elicit daily the opinion of more mature persons as to this or the other topic, and to get it all quite wrong, with a touching deference: yet when once they are tipsified by the strong wine of reviewing (with which the proficient and established reporter declines to meddle), then does all decorum depart from these striplings.

They will then prophesy pot-valiantly; they will reel in reprobation and stagger in reason; they will wallow in the vomit of their turbid sentences, thence belching forth the tetchiness and the profound distinctions of the inebriated, thence speaking maudlin praise, thence patronizing their masters beerily, thence hiccuping their misprints with a large gravity: and none living knows of their meaning. Nor, for that matter, does anybody bother to inquire. Before long, though, the managing editor, that catch-penny Argus, does observe that the unreadable is not read, and he then makes an end of this unseemly exhibit. That is the history of every literary page in every small-town paper; such is the complete saga of the reviewer's craft in our provinces: and upon the whole it ends happily.

*   *

*

But I wander from you, dear master, who have learned to quaff of this tipple in all dignity, without any open drunkenness. I speak of young failings which are alien to you, in whom I can detect indeed but two failings. For, in the first place, you did, you know, well, but you did, publish that novel. An admirer must here necessarily stammer. And I pause too to wonder that so few of you Olympians can refrain from this indiscretion. It is not apposite, it is almost shocking, for your reverers to find trudging in such lowly fields the feet of Gamaliel. Yet nearly every one of you does by-and-by publish a novel. And in every case it has led the reflective to note all its author's subsequent remarks about other persons' novels with a shaken reverence. It has led many to suspect that its author really did not know much about novel writing: and this fact (they have whispered) no professional judge of novels can afford to establish with documentary evidence. Mr. Waldo Frank, they remark, has now for a long while labored at criticism, but he has not yet succeeded in living down those novels of his late nonage, which set for him a task to baffle Methuselah. How much more fortunate (they continue) is Mr. Ludwig Lewisohn, whom nobody can ever twit about his novels, because nobody has been able to read them.

Nor is this the only consideration involved. When a hitherto so-well-thought-of Olympian as Miss Rebecca West or Mr. Edmund Wilson has brought forth a novel, both charity and common-sense have led us to concede that almost anybody might have written it; merely to write *The Judge* or *I Thought of Daisy* was, thus, condonable: yet to publish either book did seem to prove the incriminated person a poor critic of literary values. But I avoid speaking of such mysteries any further, lest I appear to prattle unreverently about the august. And of your novel also, dear master, I say, with a commensurably fine touch of scholarship, *De mortuis*—

One other failing you have exhibited, and it enabled me, I admit, to enjoy talking with you. But then an author always does, to my experience, enjoy talking with his reviewers. An author likes, most naturally, when the review has been favorable, to meet a person of marked intelligence; if to the contrary the review has belittled and excoriated, then does the author enjoy meeting its writer for less noble reasons. Let us not pry into these reasons, beyond granting the sad axiom that no sort of writing can be taken quite seriously after you have once considered the writer in person.

That is the precise point, dear master: reviewers should have no epiphany: for to find the oracle but a harmless boy, or a bald and dried up, fidgeting small fellow in nose-glasses, or a serious-minded young clumsy oaf behind large tortoise-shell spectacles—or, in brief, to find the oracle merely human—does forthwith puff up an author's so readily expansive vanity. And it was this creature (he reflects, in his blasphemy, as he

For Rhadamanthus, Smiling

gazes with far more of happiness than of venera-
tion upon the Olympian), it was this maternal
error, this ort, which spoke belittlement and
vitriol and all reprobation as to my genius!

Then is the soul of that author exalted to a
degree unbecoming the estate of an underling:
then does *hubris* possess him, so that he babbles
affably, as a man discourses with his equal. He
reveres no longer. He does not even quail. I myself, when I met Messrs. Corey Ford and Henry
S. Canby and Seward Collins, all three together,
in the clear lighting of one memorable afternoon, was not really frightened, I remember. It
is therefore in the rôle of a confessed penitent
that I declare such sacrilege ought to be avoided.
And two remedies suggest themselves. The one
is that an Olympian should go veiled among authors, the other (the more cruel perhaps, yet the
more effective way) being that at such times an
Olympian should wear upon his breast a sufficiently large mirror.

*   *

*

So far have I strayed from speaking of that triple faith which sustains you in your sublime labors. I now return to this matter. As a reviewer you must believe always, I repeat, that what you have to say is of some importance, and that it will be respectfully weighed by an audience of fair magnitude. Well, there is no human being but lives under the happy delusion that his own utterance is of importance: your task in this precinct is easy. But when it comes to the magnitude of a reviewer's audience, your faith and your imagination must, in ungracious, negligible, mere logic, be put to a strain more trying.

One confronts here a point whereon opinions are free, and free to differ. Yet two considerations stay undeniable. It is a perhaps regrettable but certain fact that the majority of persons do not ever read the literary page in the paper which they read daily: their concern is with such trivialities as the gaudier murders, the foreign outlook, or the stock market. It is another fact (amenable to much the same description) that favorable or unfavorable reviews do not remarkably alter the sales of a book; and the one thing which every publisher knows (even nowadays, when none of them any longer pretends to know everything) remains the axiom that, by and large, books "sell" in accordance with the informal criticism of word-of-mouth comment. Neither of these two considerations suggests, dear master, that millions of persons weigh your least utterance with quite that reverence which I could desire.

I deduce, instead, that the three tenets to which as a self-respecting reviewer you are committed, stay, to say the least of it, not even debatable; and here again envy awakes, flamingly, for I now covet your resemblance to the White Queen, in being able to believe three impossible things, if not always before breakfast, at any rate some time during each working day. And I debate if upon Olympus you are never visited by doubts if your labors there serve any practical end?

I know that, in my own humble sphere, I continue to wonder what may be the *raison d'être*, as the learned say, and the precise justification of book reviewing? In a country wherein so many hundreds of thousands of book reviews are published every month, it must be that this never-

idle industry supplies some national if obscure
need. Yet who profits? I demand of myself,
striking duly the pensive breast, and evoking
thence naught save the most tiny of eructations.

From his own necessarily sordid standpoint
the publisher, as I have said, perceives that the
reviewers' "free copies" of every book he pub-
lishes are an unavoidable business expense rather
than a promising investment. And the author is
beyond help. His book has been electrotyped
and distributed some weeks ago, so that, heed he
never so fondly the oracle, its reproof and advice cannot aid him now; with his ship already
at sea, he cannot well undertake to recarve more
delicately its figurehead, or to reorder the per-
sonnel of his crew, no matter what saith the god-
like voice.

As for the reading public, what are they to
make of your divine craft, dear master, when
so many oracles speak and all speak diversely?
For the omniscient do not without any excep-
tion agree: twelve times each year, let it be
noted, do those very worshipful Doctors Van
Doren and Canby, each for his own book club,
pass upon the mensual pre-eminence of our new-

est books; and in this way, upon precisely a dozen occasions annually, is the fact revealed that the one or the other errs. Rascoe is not always in harmony with Boyd; where Isabel Paterson commends, Miss Fanny Butcher may elect to live up to her surname; and one has known H. L. Mencken and Seward Collins to regard the same volume variously. When the Olympians thus disagree, they provide us with darkened counsel. So must the book buyer lack any assured guide through a jungle of tropical blurbs, because the Olympians do disagree, invariably. And what the reading public gets out of all this exalted dissension, I am sure I do not know.

*   *

*

I know only that when I look over my scrapbooks I wonder if any one of my book reviews remains worth the seven and a half cents it cost me? About the unpleasant ones I, being human, do not bother: nothing came of them; I surrender these, in enjoyable large numbers, to the oblivion which they have earned. But the columns upon columns of printed plaudits, with all those typographic huzzas, now forever pied, these trouble me. I perceive that, like Sir Andrew Aguecheek, I was adored once, and nothing seems to have come of that either. It does not seem fair that all the incense should have burned out quite as quickly as did the stink bombs.

When I published my last book, for example, did not Mr. Newton Arvin acclaim my superb humor, and Mr. Louis Kronenberger hymn my titanic genius, and Mr. Basil Davenport find in my prose style "the luxuriousness of Swinburne"? Did not Mr. Gorham B. Munson rank me, in his best scholastic manner, with "Shakespeare, Milton *et alia*"? The questions are purely rhetorical: and perhaps at this distance in time I may have quoted none of these gentlemen verbatim. Indeed, now I think of it, I believe that Mr. Davenport mistook the meaning of "luxuriousness," and Mr. Munson of "*et alia*," in a different connection. It seems so, at least. Yet I cannot understand why, when both of them make so many delightful blunders of this sort

For Rhadamanthus, Smiling

continually, I should remember these two special felicities unless I had therein some special interest. I can only hope I applauded them with no more of jealousy than befitted a generous rival in all branches of blunder-making.

However, that does not matter. My point is merely that whether the aforementioned quartet of sub-Olympians said the aforementioned things, or said quite other things, or said nothing at all, it comes at the year's end to the same sum total: it comes to nothing. My point is that all reviewing, in so far as I can see, does but corrupt, and so waste eventually, not only such minor talents, but those really considerable talents which everywhere help to manure this ever-flowering but fruitless tree of all knowledge. I observe, in short, with Andrew Lang: "Reviewing there needs must be; but how unhappy were the necessities, how deplorable the vein, that compelled or seduced a man of your eminence into the dusty and stony ways of contemporary criticism!"

It is with you a favorite topic, I note, to lament the publishing, year after year, of too many futile books by the hundreds; yet you do

89

not deplore (or, at least, not publicly) the thousands upon thousands of futile book reviews
which appear every week. You do not exhort us
(in any appropriate garb of sackcloth and ashes)
to observe that at each year's end some few of
its books survive, but that all the book reviews,
for which forests have perished, have perished
too.

All have perished, dear master, and your sublime labors are at one with the labors of Her-
cules. Along with the slain hydra and conquered
Cerberus and the cleaned stables of Augeus, oblivion has digested placidly the wit, the insou-
ciance, the erudition; the rare benevolence, the
discoverer's glow, and the lofty prophesying;
the pæans, the sarcasms, and the demolitions; the
putting of everybody (including poor old
Jehovah) in exactly his proper place; the profound comprehension of human nature, of social
conditions, of the future, and of every known
art and science; and, above all, that unswerving
infallibility to which no other being can pretend
with a straight face. At the year's end it is as
though these glories had never been. They have
passed beyond human adulation. In the back files

of magazines and of newspapers, there only, all these virtues lie disregarded, all these virtuosities rest entombed; your splendors all are faded; and of your magnanimity survives upon earth no fruitage.

People will not even remember until the crack of doom the very handsome things which you have said about my new book, and your praise of me will hardly outlast the planet. It seems a great pity.

THE FOURTH LETTER

*   *

*

STUDY IN SINCERITY

My dear Madam:

It was wholly a pleasure to receive your letter, and I look forward eagerly to the additional pleasure which I know I shall derive from your book. At the present moment, alas, those infernal eyes of mine are again out of commission, and all reading is forbidden me by the oculist. So for the while I can but think wistfully about the delights in store for

Yours faithfully,

Branch Cabell

31 September 1932

STUDY IN SINCERITY

*　　*

*

You ou have forwarded me, *my dear madam, an* advance copy of your forthcoming volume of fiction, with the suggestion that, if I "like the book," your publishers would be glad to have me write a few lines concerning it, to appear on the dust jacket. You have thus put me to the unpleasant necessity of saying I do not like your book. Your latest book appears to me to resemble each one of its predecessors in being a tedious and a meagre and a valueless performance, about which no civilized reader could say anything kindly except by lying outright.

Hardly any other exercise in the unveracious would much trouble my indurated conscience, for I find that I lie daily to preserve my quiet, my solvency, my social position, and my domestic peace. *Suppressio veri* is, in fact, the cornerstone of civility and of public concord, so that no sensitive person who dislikes being conspicuous will refrain from whoppers. Yet I cannot—it is an odd thing—lie about books with a mind wholly at ease.

That your most recent book should be refined, dependable, and dull reading-matter, after the several years which you, madam, have devoted to successful authorship, appears to me nearly an affair of necessity; and whether this particular book be much more insulse and humdrum than is the average book acclaimed by our more serious-minded readers, I am not qualified to declare. As the hair thins and the arteries thicken, one inclines to renew and to strengthen old admirations in literature, I find, rather than to adventure in new cults. I do not doubt the genius of those younger persons who succeed us, madam, in popular esteem. I remark only that their genius flourishes in fields which do not allure me. I can but wish them an excellent harvest and a civil good-bye in the same moment.

So I do not often read a modern book, and modern novels in especial I find it profitable to avoid. To adhere to this discreet course I hold as easeful to the disposition as it is improving to the mind, yet none who himself "writes" can adhere to it unmolested. One acquires friends, for instance, who "write"; and one does read their books, out of friendship, very often with an enjoyment and an interest which have not any hidebound concern with literary values. Friendship upon the whole is not so costly here as is a congenitally soft heart. For every once in a while, I find, some youngster is sure to send me a copy of his first novel, or perhaps he inflicts on me his first lean volume of inane verse-making: and into what a trap am I then betrayed by the amiability of my disposition!

It is of no least avail to write him post-haste that you have received his book and look forward to reading it with much pleasure. I have tried that method. The result was that he always wrote back to me, within the week, to ask if, now that I had read his book, would I mind giving him my candid opinion upon its merits? That method, in fine, gets you nowhere.

And besides, I can recall, even at a remove of

some twenty-five years, what a first book means
to the young man who has just written it: later,
I know, the damned thing will mean to him
something quite different; but for this blest brief
while he is proud of it. So I skim through it more
or less: I find it to be uniformly as bad as I had
feared, except in those passages which are much
worse: and yet, such is my cowardice, so complete is my more than Bourbon inability to profit
by experience, yet do I write him a civil note to
express the wholly fictitious pleasure which he
has afforded me. And every one of my polite lies
the insane whippersnapper forthwith puts into
print, out of a mistaken notion that this will
help the sales of his book. It doesn't. That is my
lone comfort in the entire affair.

For years, in brief, so often as any young author has sent me his book, just so often have I
cursed him and his impudence and both of his
misled begetters, with an embittered and sinking
heart. Thereafter, when at the dictates of imperious civility I sat down to acknowledge my
receipt of this book, I have flung truthfulness
and restraint and conscience, and all common-

sense too, to the winds. And upon the whole I shall probably continue to repeat this progression just as long as the foredoomed apprentices to our trade continue to molest me in this way. With those older practitioners whom one knows more or less intimately, it is possible to distinguish and to qualify in one's verdict, without inflicting any hurt on their reviewer-hardened sensibilities, and without straining friendship: but with the beginner I prefer not to be rational, if only because I can remember how very far from rationality is this boy in his every standard and belief and fond hopefulness. He will learn a deal better by-and-by. I prefer not to be among his many predestined instructors in disillusion.

Even more copiously (I find), when I receive one of those pathetic and ill-made books for whose printing the young ass has paid out of his own pocket, do I overflow with the milk of human kindness—which I invigorate with the alcohol of unrestrained compliment into a sort of epistolary punch. And afterward, even though he does put into type my nonsense, I have only to blush a bit, almost unrepentantly. I have enabled the preposterous nuisance to get a little more pleasure out of his dreadful book while time yet served; for the day hurries on apace, I know, when he too will see this book as it actually is. From no one of us who "write" can that dreary day be averted: each of us must read his own blunderings, by-and-by, with unglamored eyes. Still, I really do wish that this callow pest would not print my nonsense so freely, and in such very legible type too.

*   *

*

To you, madam, I need write no such besugared letter. You are not a beginning author. You have, to the contrary, published several books which proved notably successful. Each one of them has revealed, to my casual inspection, the sincere and ambitious and patient exercise of third-rate endowments: and I decline to figure, even on a dust jacket, as an admirer of that against which my auctorial life has been a protest. For the stumbling beginner I can at least cherish hope: I can regard with no hopefulness whatever the dull.

You must bear with me. It is my foible, one among a great many, to be a devotee of the niceties, of the overtones, and of the precisions of very often rewritten and suitably colored prose. I believe it well for an author to make sport with rhetorical devices, to play with vowel sounds and scansions, to build refrains, to dispose his cadences, to contrast the length of his clauses, to turn amorously to a run of liquids—to carve, as it were, his verbal cherry-stones under a magnifying glass of repeated re-inspection,—and to practise by the score yet other allied legerdemains: all quite seriously. It is but a series of microscopic parlor games, perhaps: but it will entertain him. It will lull him into the pleasure-giving illusion that the writing of prose may be an art—terse, magical, complex, fiery-hearted, and gaudy, at need, with the naïvete of a June sunset,—an art wherein, by-and-by, toward his later nineties, he may attain competence.

So at least does this putative art divert me. And I find your latest book, madam, in common with all your books, in common with most mod-

ern books, to be admirable samples of this art at
no time whatever.

Let me hasten to add that here you are at one
with your contemporaries, in so far as I may
judge, and very happily a-chime with the best
traditions of America. My main objection to our
present-day authors (as well as to their predecessors) is that they do not try to write prose commensurate with the resources of the English
language; nor do they harbor, to all appearances,
the belief that prose requires any special "writing." Prose, as an art, does not really exist to the
consciousness of our literati. It is an art in which
no American has yet excelled; and as fondly to-
day as aforetime, our best-thought-of writers
have been abetted in their clumsy and drab delinquencies by our best-thought-of reviewers. I
shall come back to that. But, in the main, reviewers do not much bother about style. At most,
they will comment, in passing, on the excellent
prose style of some author who has none. It is
what the writer "has to say" which counts: and
provided that what he says is "significant" or
"vital" or "daring" or "of grave importance"—
and, in short, is "timely,"—then his book has the

needed essentials, for everything except, of course, permanence.

*   *

*

For under the touch of time the "timely" proves always to be ephemeral. Twice, in preparing prefaces for the re-issue of a book I had written some while earlier, I have had occasion to explore the back files of the *Publisher's Weekly*: and (barring, to be sure, one's own books) I can think of no more dreadful, and yet salutary, reading for anybody who "writes." One by one they took form again, the just cloudily remembered auctorial great of yester-year. Here were Brander Matthews and John Fox and Winston Churchill and Gene Stratton Porter and Henry Van Dyke and Thomas Dixon, Jr.; Mary E. Wilkins, and Mary Johnston, and Mary Mac-Lane; Erskine, and Hergesheimer, and Cabell, and Harold Bell Wright; Upton Sinclair, and Booth Tarkington, and Henry Sydnor Harrison, and David Graham Phillips, and Richard Hard-ing Davis, and Meredith Nicholson: one had plain proof here that all these semi-fabulous persons once did actually exist.

Since each was American-born, they reached not ever to the magnitude of Hall Caine, or of Mrs. Humphry Ward, or of Michael Arlen, in the eyes of Americans, one noticed: but, even so, they had all been gravely received, at this time or the other time, as ponderable figures in our literature; and their publishers' advertising matter quoted, from the reviewers of that far-off day, encomia and prophesyings which now appeared as unbalanced and incredible and droll and dusty (and yet pathetic, too) as does the Gettysburg Address or the Apostles' Creed.

Each one of these writers, I inferred from their grim relics, was a "timely" figure. Each in his or her little hour, no doubt, wrote as to some topic or another topic in which the book buyers of that transient hour happened to be interested. So each of them (I reflected) was heard because of his or her "timely" theme; each was hymned by the reviewers and by the woman's clubs and by the advertisements now forever ensepulchered in the back files of the *Publisher's Weekly*; and

each by-and-by was to all practical intents forgotten, when the reading public turned what
might without uncustomary exaggeration be
called its mind to yet other topics.

I became quite sentimental over the back files
of the *Publisher's Weekly*. Who, I inquired,
who now remembers just what questions of the
day these mighty dead discoursed or viewed
with alarm? All these, it is plain, enchanted the
judicious briefly: but with what unrecoverable
cantraps, what ancient runes? Spoke they of race
suicide or of votes for women, of white slavery
or of the white man's burden, or of that imper-
illed younger generation which rode on bicy-
cles? What songs, in brief, did these shadowy
Sirens sing? and what good name had each hero
when he lived among club women, fondly admired upon rostra, between the Madam Chair-
man and an ice-water pitcher? Very few persons
know nowadays (I replied, to myself) and, quite
certainly, nobody living cares. When Mizraim is
become mummy he is at worst assured of a hos-
pitable reception in one or another museum; but
for the discrowned prince of literature there is
no asylum save the pulping-mill.

Special Delivery

Each one of these once popular writers, I suspect, was tainted with moral earnestness. Sincerity—"that youthful virtue," as Samuel Butler has called it—is an ill which few Americans escape in private life; and yet, incalculably, does our race demand also in its better-thought-of reading-matter that tutorial sort of dullness which voices the most subtle emotions and the most profound thoughts of morons. The fact is sad; it seems inexplicable: but it remains undeniable. So each of these aforenamed popular writers, I have no doubt, gravely addressed himself to grave problems, and had, as the phrase runs, "something to say." Each (I imagine) said his little something about "timely" matters, and duly heard his grave and apropos saying applauded: and then, of course, so soon as the especial problem concerned was settled or let slide, his saying became unrelated to reality. Each commented (I daresay) upon conditions which no longer exist; and to the intrepid explorer of their time-yellowed pages it must now seem as though these writers were talking gravely about dragons as social perils or were at pains to expose the hypocrisy of the unicorn.

Study in Sincerity

I speak with some doubt, you may observe. I do not, I confess, know to-day, if indeed I ever knew, what all these once "timely" persons did write about. Nor have I the hardihood to be myself that aforementioned explorer. For I find that I instinctively (or, at the last pinch, with plain panic terror) avoid the writer who has "something to say." He always says it so raucously, and his saying is always so very, very familiar. His admirers, happy in that their enthusiasms are not restricted by any rudiments of education, I leave free to marvel over their idol's originality: but I leave too the latter half of his book unread. I prefer the polite exercises of rhetoric.

I prefer Thackeray elegiac over the fact that all dolls are stuffed with sawdust; I prefer Sir Thomas Browne's amplification of one single truism, that Queen Anne is dead, into the gorgeous last chapter of *Urn Burial*; and I very much prefer Pater's rhapsody over La Giaconda, wherein the pomps of language triumph decisively over the absence of any particular meaning. It is my avocation to delight in the so curiously unappreciated prose of Shakespeare and the prose of Congreve, of De Quincey and of

Stevenson, of Swinburne (howsoever inde-
fensible I may here feel to be my pleasure), of
Arthur Machen and of Lord Dunsany and of
Max Beerbohm, and of yet many other writers
who have noticed that human language is an instrument far more impressive than is the human
intelligence, and so have ambitiously devoted
themselves to the nobler medium. I prefer, in
brief, a writer who knows how to write, on the
same principle that I prefer a cook who knows
how to cook, or a chauffeur who can drive a
car; and my concern with the moral earnestness
of any one of the three remains equally exiguous.

*   *

*

You, madam, I concede, are rather remarkably
in earnest; and your prose reveals, over and yet
over again, the virginal painstaking which keeps
you the delight of all assistant professors of English: nevertheless, I cannot see that your sincerity
much mitigates your dullness. I perceive only
that the two combine to make firm and enviable

your especial niche in our national letters. For I do believe you to be a permanent addition to our literature.

And yet in some respects I make bold to differ with the most of those who review your books. I have read duly their admiring remarks, my dear madam, upon your delicately chiseled style, your serene nobility, your unerring choice of the right word, and all that other bleated balderdash which proves how acceptable among us as a substitute for authentic art is your sedate hebetude. It puzzles me sometimes, I confess, to note our intense admiration for the merely inadequate: it troubles me thus to be bidden to a banquet of Lucullus when the entertainment is really modeled after a tea-party among the ladies of Cranford. And if I now and then gnash my teeth, they are, after all, my teeth.

Yet I do not, I hope, grudge you your success as a purveyor of sane and harmless and mildly edifying fiction. None can deny your somewhat muzzy admiration of the homelier virtues. One admits the whole-hearted sincerity which transfers to the pages of your books all the more tediously tender features of actual existence. One can charitably imagine that even the too long preserved virginity, whose staleness appears to permeate all your later books like a small smell, is not in the least your fault, but remains chargeable to the delinquencies of quite a number of men. All these things I at any rate concede you with an equable mind: and only when the merits of your prose style are held up for our adulation does my blood boil. Here, to be sure, I am a fanatic: and it is an ebullition, even then, far less of rage against you, madam, than of despair for my native land, which continues in this fashion to regard the third-rate with profound seriousness and respectful awe.

You really must, I repeat, bear with me. I speak pettishly, no doubt: I have cause. You are to me an unfailing bother precisely because we both dote on the unmodish idea that writing is an art demanding in its execution almost as much constant painstaking as is needed in the kitchen or in the driver's seat of an automobile. I at least am so unimaginative, so uninspired by æsthetic fervors, as to believe that all words are in the dictionary, ready for anybody's taking; and that the best writer is simply he who extracts them with the greatest discretion and rearranges them most adroitly. That is why it bothers me, madam, to see all your patient labors result in volumes which I find wholly unreadable: it is an outcome which suggests my theories may be wrong, and no male can face any such suggestion calmly.

It seems to me, in brief, that your new book, and all your books in so far as I know them, are not for my reading. I would like to like them. Yet I most obstinately don't. And it seems to me that to become ecstatic over your featureless and tidy and thin, your just wholesomely sugared and yet faintly frost-nipped manner of writing —done, as one imagines, in the best Spencerian style of the early 'eighties, with the shading and the hair lines attended to conscientiously,—is an indulgence which remains (in the teeth of all my best-loved theories) nonsense.

Yet I have tried my honest utmost to think otherwise. Time and again I have made a sortie into your writings, accompanied by hope and charity; faith, I admit, declines to be of our little

party any longer. And always I fall back re-
pulsed; always I find you invincibly dull.

*　　*

*

Very blessed are the dull: they need not seek to
inherit the earth; they already possess it. Twice
blessed are the dull in their peculiar felicity, that
they cannot ever perceive their own dullness,
or ever be convinced of its existence. As well
might a blind man be fancied to discover the
sallowness of his own complexion. Thrice blessed
are the dull in that they admire dullness with
entire sincerity. Quadruply happy are the dull
in that their numbers are strong and many.

Thus does it follow, madam, that the best-
thought-of editors, and the best-thought-of reviewers, and the best-thought-of writers of every
kind, must necessarily be dullards, without any
of them ever suspecting it, for not out of policy
and time-serving, and not, as heaven well knows,
by taking thought, do they achieve pre-emi-

nence, but solely by virtue of their innate large gifts for dullness. Such gifts, if a little cultivated through altruism and some earnestness of purpose, will enable the fatuous to admire one another with entire sincerity, and to be admired also, at a respectful remove, by the unliterary legions of book borrowers,—who revere in their reading-matter, as in every other matter, dullness, with an entire sincerity.

The dull predominate in numbers; the dull admire dullness: these are but truisms. Yet these truisms combine to explain why a great many classics in all literatures have been preserved from remote centuries. These truisms may well make of you likewise, madam, a classic. Very blessed are the dull: their lot is happy; all the fruits of earth shall be excellent and comely for them. I remark, none the less, that I do not cherish the dull, between book covers.

I can for these reasons, my dear madam, think of no fit and kindly sentiments wherewith to adorn your dust jacket save only that epitaph, slightly altered, which Joe Gargery composed, in *Great Expectations*,—"Whatsumever the failings on her part, Remember, reader, she were that good in her hart." This much I am willing to allow you: but only, be it understood, as an epitaph, in so far as I am concerned. Do not bother me any more.

THE FIFTH LETTER

*   *

*

ART, BEAUTY, AND BALDERDASH

My dear Sir:

It was wholly a pleasure to
receive your letter, and it would be
an additional pleasure to outline for
you the course of reading you have so
flatteringly requested of me, if only
I were able.   The trouble is that my
large willingness to serve you here is
counterbalanced by my entire ignorance
of the topic in which you are interested.

I am sorry -- for both our
sakes, -- and I stay

Yours faithfully,

Branch Cabell

31 September 1932

ART, BEAUTY, AND BALDERDASH

*   *

*

It was fairly pleasing, in all honesty, to hear that at forty-three (with your practice as a Doctor of Dental Surgery, I trust, thriving) your "ultimate goal is to become a profound student of literature and all the fine arts." Yet why in, as the old Spanish saying runs, the devil, should you be expecting me of all persons to outline for you "a course of reading" which will assist you toward your "ultimate goal"? Through what odd notion of me do you so perpetually write, over varying signatures and from innumerous post office addresses, to ask for that equally multiform "course of reading"?

You have been of all known professions. In age too you are desultory, ranging from seventeen, as a sophomore, even into your seventies, as the librarian of an athletic club. In this last-

named avatar, it comes back to me, I suspected
you of being likewise a dealer in rare books and
autographs, and I guessed rightly. Sometimes,
as to-day, you wish to absorb all "art," at other
times your interest narrows down to literature,
and then again you need only the best books
about Provençal poetry, or about phallic worship, or about the Rosicrucians; I have known
you to specialize on Merlin, and on Villon, and
on Marlowe, and on crystal gazing, and on the
Wandering Jew, and on Roland (the paladin,
not the statesman), and on the Ballard family,
and on Russian folk-lore, and, once at least, on
the Man in the Moon; very often you want a
complete course in pornography, and yet more
often do you require tuition in black magic: but
always, my dear imbecile, you assume both my
loving-kindness and my leisure to be unlimited.

Neither, I can assure you, is anything of the
sort. Necessity denies me the time to bother with
you; nor does my philanthropy prompt me, by
ordinary, to set up as a private tutor for the
public. Yet, as it happens, your letter asking for
a list of "the most helpful books about æsthetics"
reaches me as I finish reading still another book

concerning æsthetics; and my thoughts turn to a
more or less related incident.

*   *

*

Because of my own peccadillos in print I was
privileged no great while ago to attend a gather-
ing of some forty professional writers under
frankly educational auspices. We responded, it
may be, to our auspices. In any case, affairs had
reached the stage called "an open discussion"
of I never discovered just what, and the refrain
of our morning-long liturgy stayed constant.

One after another these somewhat strange
looking persons—for authorship, whatever it
may do for the mind, does not beautify the body
—arose and coughed. Thereafter each so defer-
entially cleared throat spoke with dauntless conviction of our duty,—of our multifold duties to
the public, to art, to altruism, to posterity, to
the American spirit (for it was generally agreed
that our masterworks ought to be "autochtho-
nous"), and I even heard two elderly persons of

my own obsolete generation dwell upon our
special duty toward that free-handed Deity who
had blessed us with special talents. It all sounded
most handsomely, and it made the business of
writing any salable form of reading-matter seem
a high-minded and painful pursuit wherein only
seers and martyrs might hope to excel.

I listened, I admit, in extreme melancholy begotten by low envy of such elevated sentiments.
My reflection was that for some reason or another such sentiments quite obviously caused
their expounder's socks to wrinkle and to slide
yet more downward, the higher that his moral
fervor aspired. In the while that I wondered over
this phenomenon the young woman who sat
beside me remarked sotto voce, "But I write
because I like to!"

I looked at that intelligent young woman with
instant affection. I was cheered at once, to my
heart's core, by this plaintive small heresy, which
had made me feel no longer signal in irresponsi-
bility and low-mindedness. I became charitable.
I perceived that at any rate the most of my confrères were talking so much sonorous nonsense
out of a general notion that it was expected of

them under our present auspices. But I said only, in confidence to my new-found friend, "Me too!"

* *

*

More than once since then have I been reminded of this brief incident, when I set about reading any book upon the nature and aim of æsthetics. For I find that every American who writes or speaks publicly about æsthetics inclines to a great deal of magniloquent balderdash. It is expected of him by a high-minded and serious citizenry. He must justify "art" upon some altruistic or moral ground, very much as did my confrères exalt our trade of writing to the plane of self-sacrificing duty. He must rank the artist somewhere between the seer and the martyr, and yet suggest too that the artist's labor has kinship with the public-welfare work of the local chamber of commerce. He must always ignore the fact that the artist pursues his art, in chief, because—as my comely savior put it—"he likes to."

It follows that time and again the American
reader, during his half-impressed and half-restive
progress through a book upon æsthetics, finds
himself lugged toward the gray and barren up-
lands of duty. This is a fact, I imagine, which in
itself goes very far to explain our artistic back-
wardness. To be told thus constantly how and
why and with what thoroughness you ought to
assimilate art and beauty, and how much real
good they will do you, stays to my finding, at
any rate, as unappetizing as a discourse upon the
dietary value of spinach or of turnip salad. It
provokes, somehow, an irrational dislike of the
proffered fare.

Nor will the American pundit in his approach
to æsthetic matters refrain from wholly lucid
illogic. I speak, it may be, in wrath and extreme
fretfulness. Yet no prose writer could be expected to view with oyster-like equanimity the
pronouncement I discover in a recent book of
this sort: "Poetry, fiction, and drama use a common material, language, and therefore a study of
any one of the three is also an examination of
the nature of the other two." The author (it
really does seem incredible, and I can but ask

you to take my word for it) then discusses poetry upon the assumption that he is thus disposing of all literature and all drama. This feat do I find performed by an accepted "authority" upon æsthetics, in a three dollar book, brought out by an established and even venerable publishing firm.

Well, but let us paraphrase this. Weddings, christenings, and funerals use a common material, the prayer book; and therefore a study of the nature of marriage is also an examination of the nature of death. The reasoning appears to me the same, and the deduction equally fallacious. For the considerate person the broad gap between the sophomorics of poetry and the refinements of intelligent prose is not to be bridged by stating that both Edgar A. Guest and George Jean Nathan employ "language." And to declare that the material of acted drama also is "language" appears rather like asserting that a suit of clothes is made of buttons. The buttons and the dialogue are components, but they are noticeably remote from being the entire material. You have but to resort to your radio this very evening to perceive how far does the broadcasting of any play (which preserves all the "language") differ from your witnessing an acted drama in its fit theatre.

The confusion here, I imagine, sprang in large part from that superstitious lip-service which we yet render to "poetry." I would not belittle "poetry"—in, I mean, verse form, wherein true poetry can now flourish but as an acorn thrives in a flower pot. I protest, to the contrary, that in my time I have got more than enough pleasure from verse to leave me eternally grateful. I remark only that versified poetry is for the young, although it can of course be composed, with entire sincerity, by the mentally immature at all ages. It is excellent for a writer to begin by writing verse, just as every primitive civilization has begun by writing verse; but he too ought to grow out of it into some control, where there are no absolute masters, of the more subtle and complex and communicative, and the more musical, art of prose. I mean, in fine, that when anyone over twenty-five approaches me to talk gravely about "poetry" the effect is much as though he had approached me on roller skates. He may not be insane; he may even be justified:

but to my mind he has perturbingly failed to put
away childish things, and I feel far more comfortable when he leaves me.

*   *

*

From this excursus I return, with entirely respectful admiration, to the last book I have read
concerning æsthetics. And I find it depressing.
This scholarly thesis, I observe, is well considered, it is sage (as sage, that is, as any gravely
designed book about æsthetics can hope to be), it
is thorough, and it is competently done. I have
read every line of it with unflagging interest. So
far as the book goes, I applaud, if that matters,
heartily. Yet I observe in it one defect, an enor-
mous defect.

For I find that in the outcome I have read all
these pages, along with thousands of other pages,
in an ever-foiled hope of finding by-and-by
some direct statement as to why an artist pursues his art. "The creative impulse," I read here,
"has been traced by many writers to have a social

origin, as arising from the desire to communicate to others what the artist experiences. But"—for here again sounds the martyr motif—"but to attribute the herculean labors and sufferings of the creative minds of the ages to such a trite purpose indicates a most naïve conception of the nature of human experience, and a disregard, to say the least, of the records of artistic history."

In yet another passage I find pointed out the axiom that art is not "actuated by a desire to please . . . Genius does what its nature compels it to do, irrespective of consequences." And again I read: "The artist can no more give a reason for his works than he could for his life. His work is his life and his reason for living."

—All which is very well and wholly true, so far as it goes. Yet it does not go far beyond triteness, yet all these dicta approach without ever quite touching the dodgèd truth that every artist pursues his art in chief because he enjoys that pursuit, just as unexplainedly (to the opinion of some of us) as other zealots enjoy the pursuit of a fox or of a golf ball.

It is in each case an indulgently regarded form of time-wasting. The large difference is that nobody pretends that the fox hunter or the golf player is actuated by his strong sense of duty or by altruism or by any other moral motive. His sports are lightly appraised, by relatively un-biased persons. But most books about æsthetics emanate from the professional art critic or the professional artist—of whom neither is at liberty to question the importance of art without im-pugning thereby his sole excuse for existing and the honesty of his livelihood. Mere self-respect will implant in him an heroic predisposition against cutting off his next year's income.

It follows that mankind has but infrequent prompters to face the triviality of any finished art product—whether it be a picture or a sonnet or a symphony—in human existence. It follows that (to the best of my limited knowledge) in no book about æsthetics is the fact dwelt upon that if every existent work of art could be dumped into the Pacific Ocean next Monday morning, the most of us would be jogging on quite com-fortably by Tuesday afternoon.

*   *

*

I do not mean only that inestimable millions lead gratifying and useful lives without devoting any instant therein to "art." It requires but a moment's frankness to see that "art" takes no important part in the life of a solid and reliable citizen, howsoever cultured. The merchant prince, the lawyer, and the bootlegger, in common with the butcher, the baker, and (if he still thrives) the candlestick maker, must perforce pass days hand-running untroubled by any consideration of "art." To each of these national bulwarks, all "art" remains but an occasional stopgap for some vacant hour when there is no business of real importance in hand: to each of these, the more trite, the more nugatory, and the more readily comprehensible exercises of "art" are the more congenial, as necessitating the least mental effort; and for no self-respecting tax-payer, at the year's end, does the time which he has devoted to "art" equal the time he has spent at the telephone or in the bathtub.

It may be objected, of course, that how much time he, and yet other persons, devote to "art," and how much to bathing and telephoning, is a ratio of no large interest or significance. Intensity, and not duration, I have heard it whinnied, tests the delight and satisfaction derived from "art." There are in our lives certain thrilling moments which we never forget, and most of these moments we owe to "art," you may remind me.

I am afraid so at least, because so very many excellent people do talk just this sort of nonsense. And for my part, I cannot but marvel at the creature who speaks in this fashion. It is quite as though (you might imagine) this prattling and grave blockhead had never known the great commonplaces of his life here as a thinking animal: had never clung to the soft and warm and bulging body of his mother for protection against his childhood's terror of darkness; had got no delight from the awkward kisses of first love; had entered no maiden ruthlessly in the while that her young face, so close to his face, wore that fond look of agony and submissive gratitude; had never felt the hand of his own child cling uncertainly to his hand for the first time; and had not ever looked upon the aloof strange sleeping of any beloved dead. It is, for that matter, as though this prattler had never tasted food when he was actually hungry.

Otherwise, he would not speak thus zany-like as to those thin and feeble tinglings which "art" trickles costively into its patronizer's but half-engaged consciousness. He would not talk of these as being in any well-rounded human life an important element, or as having power to compete with the commonplace and sublime moments which I have but indicated from among so many other moments,—those moments in which every man has felt (with a sudden kindling, with an unexplained exultance which finds his happiness or his fear or his sorrow alike splendid) that all his faculties are now engrossed, and that all his bodily and mental and spiritual being is in full use, and that all the volatile flame of his living is crowded now into one tiny point of incandescence, concentered, devouringly, intolerably.

One simply does not derive any such moments from considering a picture or a sonnet or a symphony: one does derive them from the great animal commonplaces of every human life over and yet over again. You have merely to compare the *Œdipus Tyrannus* with the circumstance that some day a mortician will pump you

full of embalming fluids, in order to compre-
hend that Sophocles did but fiddle with the
tragic, just as you have only to go to bed with a
desirable young woman to perceive at once that
the love music of *Tristran und Isolde* is an irrelevant blather.

So the considerate person will admit frankly,
I think, that every exercise of "art" is but a stopgap for some vacant hour, and a most trivial
matter, in so far as "art" at all enters the life of
any solid and reliable citizen at wide intervals.
Nor is it, very happily, anything save yet more
balderdash to esteem that these scattered moments given up to "art" can infect and permeate
the remaining hours of professional and family
life. The emotions roused by contemplating an
æsthetic masterpiece are shallow: as chalk with
cheese, so do they compare in gusto with any
private personal emotion. And after all, they
turn out to be so beneficently transient that we
are not operated upon by surgeons who are
thinking meanwhile about Beethoven; the
plumber does not waste yet additional time in
our lavatories by discussing Proust with his
helper; and a board of directors is but rarely

heartened during the official passing of a dividend (or, so at least I am informed) by any devotion to Leonardo da Vinci.

* *

*

Even so (I can fancy your replying, my dear sir, out of that inexhaustible fund of balderdash which we hold axiomatic), even so, art means everything to the artist: we agreed but now that art is his life and his reason for living; him at least this loss of all art's masterpieces would provide with an unpacific Tuesday. Such winged words I can homerically imagine to pass the barrier of your teeth, as you speak bosh, with that healthy glow of self-approval which this exercise usually kindles.

Yet by the practising artist, I admit, the time devoted to art is considerable. I admit, too, that the pursuit of his art is to him an affair of supreme and very much exaggerated importance. My point is merely that the importance of each finished work of art to the artist also remains small. That is natural: it is even unavoidable. To achieve competence in any art one must hammer away at it unremittingly, at least twenty-five hours to the day, so that no artist can afford an actual interest in any one of those other various arts which ordinarily figure in mural paintings as overfed females in tunics. He may quite harmlessly affect, of course, some such interest, and he often does. I have known in fact three excellent writers who pretended to appreciate music, just as I have met few musicians who did not admit him- or her-self to be an authority upon literature, as well as, for that matter, everything else.

But I pause here. I reflect upon the loud omniscience of most musically gifted persons, and it prompts me to confine myself to my own bailiwick of spoilt paper and tinkling typewriters. *Non ultra*, I remark in my pedantic way, after a few moments of sedate reflection, *crepidam*.

I know then, but too well, that every noteworthy professional writer, in addition to his necessitated ignorance of all the arts save literature, very rarely ever reads anything. The trouble is, I suspect, that when once he has mastered his trade, in so far as his talents permit, then the acknowledged masterpieces of literature, for the most part, must appear to him either too childishly conceived, or else too ill executed, to evoke more than an antiquarian interest. And, of course, he regards with a vivid and thinly veiled abhorrence the writings of those fellow practitioners who are yet alive. Of this latter truth at least I am wholly certain, because I have survived some thirty years of hearing authors talk about their contemporaries.

I know, too, that no conscientious writer can look upon his own finished books with much less abhorrence, in the light of their multitudinary flaws and shortcomings, which he, ill-fated, is doomed to perceive more clearly than may the most callow and unsympathizing reviewer. And from no one of these known facts can I deduce that any writer who is worthy of consideration could possibly object to having all literature, along with all other works of art, dumped into the Pacific Ocean next Monday morning.

I admit, though, that in each writer's heart a trace of tenderness lingers for the plaything which he has most recently completed in book form. Even though he might pay the postage on it as far as California, he would not convey that book thither in person. That book as yet remains near and in some sort stays a part of him— to whom it seems that all other books with his name upon their covers were written, and were very badly written, by somebody else. Yes, that last book, which he himself wrote, appears in its own little way to be well enough. But the writer's real interest and the real incentive of his continued living is that unfinished bit of phrase-shaping which he keeps yet in hand and on account of which he labors heart-breakingly (just as labors the fox hunter or the golf player) "because he likes to."

I believe that every other artist in every other field of æsthetics is about his inconsequential play there for exactly the same reason. I believe that no existent books about æsthetics can much help you, my dear sir, toward your "ultimate goal," because none of them, in so far as I know, can refrain from at any rate implying (precisely as did my confrères) that every at all notable artist is the victim of exalted ideals and a strong sense of duty.

I believe that, to the contrary, the artist alone of mankind is rewarded for doing what he most wants to do, simply and quite selfishly, "because he likes to." And I believe that nobody ought to gloss over, with slick platitudes, this wholly irrational liking, since I take it to be the origin of all art, of all man-created beauty, and (as the uncivil may observe I have demonstrated) of considerable balderdash.

THE SIXTH LETTER

* *

*

UPON SECOND THOUGHT——

My dear Sir:

It was wholly a pleasure to
receive your letter, even though I
can but reply that an agreement with
my publishers restricts the inscribing
of my books to the signing of the
regular autographed editions. I am
sorry. It would be a real and a very
deep pleasure, after the many kindly
things which you have said about my
work, to inscribe your first editions,
but as matters stand I have no choice
in the affair.

Yours faithfully,

Branch Cabell

31 September 1932

UPON SECOND THOUGHT —

*   *

*

$\mathcal{Y}$ou, my dear sir, who write to me with such handsome expressions, write entirely too often. You are (for epistolary purposes, at least) a whole-hearted admirer of my books, as to the merits of which you speak in terms that I myself could not heighten. Of these books, it develops later in your letter, you possess one or two "first editions"; so you desire me "to inscribe with some word of personal greeting," and to autograph for you, each of these first editions. More often than not, as happens to-day, the books themselves have arrived synchronously with the fervid letter wherein you thank me in advance for granting you this favor, which (you lead me to infer) will brighten your entire future existence.

Now, in the first place, of each of the four

volumes you ask me to inscribe, my publishers
issued a definitive text, in a limited number
of signed copies at, to be sure, a somewhat higher
price than that asked for the regular trade edition. These copies could be had through any
book dealer, at this increased price. Of these
facts you are wholly aware. I am thus forced,
after reading your letter, to debate: whether you
esteem my autograph as an inutility which upon
the whole you would like to have, but did not
think worth the additional two dollars and a
half? or whether you approach me as an easily
gulled prig from whom glib flatteries can thrift-
ily obtain a signed inscription for each of your
four volumes gratis?

Yet, upon second thought, I perceive that I
wrong you. You have already invested fifty
cents in postage for the forwarding and the return of your books. It is thus made mathemati-
cally evident that you do at least esteem my
autograph at twelve and a half cents, which is
better than nothing, I grant, but remains an
evaluation from which I can extract no large
personal compliment. It is an evaluation, too,
which I cannot quite reconcile with your epis-

tolary expressions of reverence and delight, nor with a deal of toplofty talk about your undying gratitude and your cloudless future, did you but possess a book by me autographed. To be made utterly happy for the rest of one's life, I cannot but reflect, would seem to be worth two dollars and a half: yet here is one who esteems otherwise, and seeks bliss at a discount.

In fact I regard with perplexed admiration all the ways of the book collector, and I have learned to receive his monstrously civil letters (such as yours, my dear sir, which I protest is mighty handsomely phrased) without finding therein any firm ground for self-elation. For I am taking it for granted you are really a book collector.

Lost souls yet infest this earth, let me whisper, who pretend to be book collectors; who write just such letters as yours to accompany the first editions which they too forward; and who plan to profit deceivingly. So black is the wickedness of these persons that (when once the great-hearted and guileless author has written the desired "word of personal greeting," and has signed his full name to it too, in each book,

smirkingly) then they design to peddle, before
the auctorial ink has well dried, to peddle at the
nearest book store and at an enhanced price these
very volumes, as being "presentation copies" and
gifts tendered by the author to some cherished
friend. Thus exceedingly black, beyond the
nigritude of ebony or of midnight or of carrion
crows, is the great wickedness of these persons;
and thus have they dealt with me, more than
once.

But I avert from such infamies, taking you to
be none of these rogues. I assume that you are
really a book collector; I assume your honesty
and your good faith in a proper fraction of your
remarks: and I remain unpuffed-up.

*   *

*

To be collected by virtuosi is no doubt flatter-
ing. If I speak here with some taint of uncertainty, it is but because I observe that this tribute
remains an honor not yet accorded me nor any
other known author. Under the rules of the

book collector's strange if harmless pastime one
hunts first editions, preferably in the "first state,"
wherefrom has been removed no scar of the
printers' slips, slight misdemeanors, nor rank
aberrancies. To the collector any later issue, into
which the author has foisted a text free of misprints, becomes virtually worthless. I deduce
(with whatsoever unwillingness) that it is the
contribution of the book's compositors rather
than of the book's writer which is valued by all
players at the strange game of book collecting,—
who in the pursuit of their pastime can at best
pay to any "collected" author the equivocal
compliment of preferring his work in the shape
farthest removed from his intentions.

For the author too, you see, may have his
hobby: and should the demented fellow elect (as
Keats has approximately phrased it) to sway
about upon his hobby horse and think it Pegasus,
there is no great harm done. I do not know that
upon the whole he is much happier for having
this sort of equestrianship observed and applauded by the cognoscenti who esteem his
books according to the ratio of their misprints.
I am sure that he is often thrust into a most deli-

cate predicament when he finds his books valued by the "collector" not only for their typographical errors but for still other qualities wherein the author does not desire pre-eminence.

For do you but observe his plight! All courtesy is a draft to be honored in its own coinage. He could prefer, certainly, some compliment of a more congenial and more rational nature. Even so, the applause has a pleasant ring; and the applauder seems sincere. Not every one of us is ready in such circumstances to snub adulation, as did Wellington so perfectly, with the crisp reply, "Don't be a fool!" In fact, to make just that reply to a dissertation upon one's own genius would appear uncivil; and yet one really is tempted to make it, now and again, to the undesired disciple.

I do not mean that you, my dear sir, I would thus hortate. I mean, rather, that when some years ago the Society for the Suppression of Vice first brought me before the public as the writer of "an obscene and lewd and lascivious and indecent book," its well-meant endeavors established me in far too wide estimation as an approved pundit of pornography. The legend lives on, in astounding tenaciousness, without requiring any least further nurture; and I still suffer from the admirers thus attracted. This very morning, for example, I received, along with your dithyrambs and your four books, a letter from yet another book collector. After the customary encomia of my writings which ordinarily bespeak the asking of a more or less unreasonable favor by return post, he requests me to select from my complete works "the most lively passage of an erotic nature" from which a drawing could be made to serve as his book plate.

It is not in the least his fault that, about the corners, my mouth is still faintly frothing. The man honestly intends a compliment; he writes too as a person of fair culture: and yet, somehow, to find my books regarded as a thesaurus of all fornications does not seem to me utterly complimentary. Not ever, not even after twelve years of whole-hearted encouragement by the obnoxious, have I learned to think of myself as a connoisseur of copulation: and so when I receive, as I continue to receive, some dozen letters a month (the most of them from professed book collectors) fiddling with this eternal stale theme, I do not love all my professed admirers. I love, rather, the first Duke of Wellington.

It would be well, I reflect, could these morons and young bitches take coition more quietly. I admit, though, that this task has always baffled Americans as a nation, and that American literature in especial has remained singularly unaffected by the persiflage of the drawing-room. That seems particularly true to-day when, under the lime-light of a perfervid and defiant "frankness," the genital organs are put through their limited repertory in so very many quite inexplicably popular books. The shrill emphasis and the visible excitement of the author hereabouts (just as formerly did the abashed utterance and the virginally vague hints of the author hereabouts) really do lead you to surmise, in either instance, that his social advantages have been somewhat restricted. In neither instance, I mean, is it in the least the tone of the contemporaneous gentry, to whom these matters have always seemed merely amusing.

One encounters nowadays so many scathing

dicta as to "the genteel tradition" in American
letters that I rather hesitate to suggest that
the true "genteel tradition" has at all times
remained unrepresented there. I content myself
with pointing out that the majority at any rate
of our writers have been (to employ a quaintly
old-fashioned term) not quite ladies and gentlemen. I say only that, in consequence, to speak of
any sexual relationship has tended to flurry
American writers, either to the extreme of regarding the matter as undiscussable or to the
other extreme of regarding coition as a very
gravely important matter, such as well justified
coarse speaking and a deal of heavy-handed
sociology.

Yet all the while, I believe (but beyond doubt,
during the last thirty-five years), their relatively
civilized social betters, in unliterary drawing-
rooms, have spoken of sex as a mildly pleasant
joke and have continued to discuss its gymnastics
in this particular aspect. Such, I can assure the
literati, has for a long while been the attitude of
the upper classes. That is the true "genteel tradition" as to all erotic matters; it is a tradition not

yet represented in American letters; and it is also a tradition which causes me to fidget before those who gravely collect my books as erotica. I designed those books for quite other purposes.

*   *

*

But the request of your fellow collector, my dear sir, has led me into some remoteness from the matter of inscribing your first editions. I return to it. Now that each of my books has been revised, for the last time, and fitted each into its appointed place in what I take to be the continuous story of one sole life, these first editions have lost, to my finding, any individual existence. They seem—to me, at least—but the sketches for various chapters of a book which since these various chapters were outlined has been finished. Only in the eighteen volumes which contain the finally revised and augmented and co-ordinated text of the Storisende Edition of my books do I find my own writing in its completed form; and

Upon Second Thought ——

I tend frankly to regard all other books with my full name on the cover as uncanonical.

Even though upon second thought I may not exactly disown as my work these earlier versions, and though I extend my complaisance to the point of accepting royalties upon their regrettably small sale, yet beyond this I am adamant. The artist retains his quirk of honor. I must wholly disclaim, I find—wholly and in all gravity —these incomplete and incompletely linked-up first sketches as my own finished work. Such work I detect only in the Storisende text of my collected writings: and in my private meditations I can accept these eighteen volumes alone as being actually by, or at any rate as actually completed by, me.

—All which I mention as of no earthly importance, my dear sir, either to you or to anyone else, but as necessarily affecting the point of view from which I regard the various some-and-fifty volumes which in my time I have seen through the press. It is a point of view which allows me to see the finally revised versions alone. It is a point of view which compels me to see in

your request a large amount of impertinence. I
shall come back to that.

*　　*

*

Meanwhile the élite who "collect" have their
special grievance in this matter. They tell me
it remains among book collectors (through an
extension of that principle by which first editions
and "first states" are valued) an open question
whether, when a book is once published, the author may wisely, or indeed with strict honesty,
prepare and issue a revised version. To the collector, I hear (and I hear it rather often), a revised version is neither one thing nor the other;
its claim to rank as a first edition stays debatable;
to have to purchase it is a nuisance, yet without
it one's collection becomes not impeccantly
complete.

Now hereabouts (upon second thought) I
somewhat fervently sympathize with the collector's grievance. It seems to me that the purchaser

of a book's original version, whether or not he be a collector, may entertain most naturally a belief that, after any outlay of solid cash, his copy of this book, as rationally as his radio set or his motor car, should in plain justice belong to him forever unbelittled by the knowledge that others possess a later model of the same chattel. So extremely general and human is this feeling that one, I now recall, can always obtain a friendly hearing in the quaint circles which discuss literature—and may indeed acquire an inexpensive air of critical acumen—by remarking that the revisions have quite spoiled the book. Very often in such earnest company have I thus dismissed Henry James or George Moore or some yet other patient deviser of irritating improvements with whom I had no special sympathy. I spoke, to the best of my knowledge and ability, balderdash: but it provoked, I observed, only the most cordial and grave agreement.

Nevertheless, my dear sir, from the point of view of a book's author, if he happen to take his art seriously, and to desire for it no less than perfection, here is no question at all in this mat-

ter of revised editions. It is plain, for example,
that to have written and published what in general opinion stays the supreme masterwork of
English literature would lull any rational person
into some pleased repose upon supereminent
laurels. It is equally plain, after consulting the
two subsequent revised editions of *Hamlet*, that
Shakespeare did not think so. Nor is it certain
to the obsessed artist that Shakespeare was always an imbecile. The erratic creature will condone, he will even emulate Shakespeare in this
matter of piddling revisions. No more than the
aforementioned Henry James or George Moore,
no more than Tennyson, no more than Pater,
no more than Sir Thomas Browne, no more than
Edward Fitzgerald left unmolested the *Rubáiyát*,
will the incurable artist in letters ever leave well
enough alone.

Instead, with the same callousness which leads
him to ruin a most desirable "first state" by making the text coherent and legible, he will further-
more presume to make the text better. That
perfection which is his goal he can never attain:
and even he knows this much, somewhat over

clearly. Yet, through experience, through study, through repeated trial, and through a most damnable deal of trouble-taking, he may come to fall short of perfection by a margin appreciably less. To do that is his main aim in life: it is also, I believe, his main pleasure: and in his pursuit of it the besotted drudge has not time to think about the annoyance he is creating for the collector by thus flooding the book market with so many variants of the same volume.

*   *

*

Not for the half-twinkling of an eye, my dear sir, could anyone upon second thought defend such conduct. It is akin a bit too remotely to altruism and far too nearly to time-wasting. It is an over-busy unthrift; and it is also a puttering which deludes not even its own practitioners.

Myself, for example, I look with sad wonder at this spick-and-span "first state" of a volume of short stories as it was published by me in

1905, which you have forwarded for my signature and my "word of personal greeting." I recollect with what moil and swinking these tales were made ready for their first printing in magazine form near thirty years ago; with what, as it were, operosity they were all revised in 1905 for their début between these gaudy book covers; with what long labors they were rewritten to make their third appearance, a decade and a half later, in the brown Kalki binding; with what painstaking they were refashioned into rather more subtle forms, about eight years afterward, for their inclusion in the sage-green Storisende set; and incidentally with what shaky persistence I then signed some sixteen hundred copies of this special volume, in my extreme illness, propped up among pillows, and sustained with large doses of sweetened whisky, hour after hour, through the length of four August days. I recollect all these matters, I repeat: and I recollect also the Horatian fable of the mountain which after prolonged birth-pangs produced a mouse.

Thereafter I look, in very well contented self-derision, from your copy of the 1905 version toward the Storisende version of this book, and toward all the other so often reconstructed and repolished volumes of the Storisende. Edition. In no case does it seem to me, after an instant of second thought, that from any practical point of view the outcome, in the form of any one of those tall green books, justifies the years of expended toil. Yet it does seem to me that in each successive version each volume was consistently improved; I am certain that, in an unhilarious and hermitical way, I enjoyed the making of each revision; and I most firmly believe that (always in the special sense and for the illogical reasons which I have set forth in another place) the main end of all art is to divert the artist. He, like the book collector, must be about his own strange and harmless pastime: and I doubt if either upon second thought could tell you why.

But I think too that each ought to go about his nonsense, my dear sir, without annoying the other. Not poignantly have you annoyed me by your unconcealed preference for the earliest written of my books in its crude "first state," bedizened and aglare with its equally crude reproductions of Howard Pyle's flamboyant pictures: I can well understand that you are not concerned with the merits either of the text or of the illustrations, but collect books much as boys collect postage stamps or birds' eggs, for no reason at all. Yet you do annoy me slightly. For I—and I too for no reason at all—have given over a largish number of years to revising this same text, in accordance with my own just as irrational hobby. It would be to pile an Ossa of self-contradiction upon a Pelion of time-wasting, did I now formally acknowledge and sign this long-ago disowned preliminary draft, and even enhance its market value (by the terms of your own frank computation) to the amount of twelve and a half cents. I cannot quite get out of my mind the suspicion that it is wrong of you to tempt me to these excesses.

I can see, in short, no least reason for me to inscribe any autographed inanities in these four books, and thus brighten your entire future existence. We who follow after any such idiotic hobbies as you and I affect, my dear sir, do not merit terrestrial bliss. That is a truism so self-

evident, and in its own way so edifying, as to
compel any pious person, upon second thought,
to return your books precisely as they came to
me. I have not even cut the pages of the two that
were issued untrimmed.

THE SEVENTH LETTER

＊　　＊

＊

GRACE ABUNDANT

My dear Friend:

It was wholly a pleasure to
receive your letter, and I appreciate
the many delightful things which you
say therein, although for my soul's
health I must endeavor not to take
them too seriously.

I am sorry that your letter
comes just as we are leaving home
for an indefinite stay, but once we
are settled down I shall hope to
reply to you at greater length.

Yours faithfully,

Branch Cabell

31 September 1932

GRACE ABUNDANT

* *

*

*W*hensoever *you write to offer your affec-*
tions, with all the usual extra-legal privileges, my
dear child, I am afraid that, for just one instant,
at the bottom of my heart, your letter pleases
me. I doubt not that during my reading of it I
smirk. All men are thus fashioned to begin with;
and I have not noted that the pursuit of literature
wholly eradicates masculine vanity. Then, after
I have finished your letter, I drift into being a
little sorry for you, and in some part, somehow,
for myself.

A great many strange women (not all of
whose steps, I trust, take hold on hell) still favor
me with strange letters, though it seems a long
while since any one of them has raised a really
fresh topic. Of these women, who are in mental
matters as mature as they will ever be, I have

spoken elsewhere: and inasmuch as you have read "every one of my books," I let drop the trite tale of their aberrations. But now and again you also write to me in more naïve terms, upon stationery of widely varying color and quality, and from all quarters of the United States; and I do rather wonder at you.

This morning, I find, you are in your final year at college. Your name is Grace: your papa is a rural mail carrier, on a sixty-mile route, and has himself written many unpublished poems. Only two of them have been printed, under a nom de plume, in your local paper, and of these two poems you are so kind as to send me no copies. You have in this world only your twenty years of existence; an intense admiration of my books, which has led you really to understand my inmost nature; a rather nice black dress for evening wear, with turquoise embroideries on the sleeves; a suit of blue silk pajamas, your membership in the Methodist Church, which you design to abandon, and three lipsticks; two short stories, on their way back to you from two magazines; a desire to write five novels, of which the outlines are quite clear in, as one might say, your mind; the intention of attending a school of journalism; a part-time job, at eight dollars a week, selling calico at the Bon Marché; two dollars and twenty-five cents in coin of the Republic, one Canadian dime, and three Chinese coppers with square holes in their centres.

Upon these miscellaneous possessions do you base, somehow, the plan as to which you write me, sitting upon the steps of Chancellor Hall, where you can see only pine-trees, which have a delightful smell, and are your pine-trees, because nobody else can see them just now. And if I agree to your plan, you promise, in your own words, "not to have a baby."

*   *

*

My child, I really wonder at you! It is known to you, of course, that we literary men, like royal personages of a more picturesque régime, possess our mistresses *en titre* and our private *parcs aux cerfs*, quite apart from our caprices with the most brilliant of lady novelists (our intrigues

with the feminine reviewers coming rather under
the head of business needs), our amourettes with
the fair and febrile daughters of the idle rich,
and our passing alliances with the more famous
queens of Hollywood. You know, in brief, that
we flourish in just the atmosphere of a *Saturday
Evening Post* serial, shrugging lightly (over exotic foods and rare vintages) at Casanova de
Seingalt as a prude, at Sardanapalus as a skinflint.
Is it not plain to you then, from these known
facts, how quizzically all my confrères in this
atmosphere would of necessity regard the spec-
tacle of an as-yet-Methodist schoolgirl approaching my bedchamber in a black dress with turquoise embroideries on the sleeves, carrying
under her arm a suit of blue silk pajamas?

I admit that in person you may be well
enough. You tell me at least that you are five
feet and two inches in height, weigh one hundred and twelve pounds, with but one mole on
your entire body, and that you have brown hair
which curls naturally, large eyes of a battleship
gray color, and a complexion so perfect that
(despite those lipsticks) you "use very *little*
make-up, if any at all." These specifications

sound appetizing. Nevertheless, my child, in
your black dress with turquoise embroideries on
the sleeves, would you cut not but an unimpres-
sive and even a droll figure in that glittering long
line of most lovely ladies *en grande toilette*
which forms every evening at my front door,
extending across the formal garden and through
the park gates, down Monument Avenue and
well around the corner into Cleveland Street?
Did you but once hear them wrangling like par-
roquets with the tall traffic policeman, Sergeant
Hagan, who affably keeps this fair mob in order
until I have made my sedate choice, it would
trouble you, I think, to observe with what open-
ness these fine women of the world court my
embraces. Me, at all events, it would trouble,
very greatly, did a glance out of my library window ever reveal any such phenomena.

That is why I mildly resent (and yet enjoy,
too) a marked tendency among my female correspondents to rank me somewhere between
Nero and the town bull. From at least one standpoint, it is a compliment, which, as my age in-
creases, becomes yet more emphatic. From another standpoint, I am not deeply interested in

perverse pleasures and strange sins (to adhere to the quaint Victorian description of sports familiar to most schoolboys), nor may the more gross and terrible delights of black magic appeal to me any longer with an irresistible lure; at orgies I go to sleep far more quickly than at church; and I do rather feel, at the bottom of my heart, that adultery and seduction begin to rank almost with progressive euchre and tiddledewinks.

It is no doubt an effect of failing animal heat: but after fifty one does come to perceive in all these splendid matters a strong flavor of silliness. One reflects in brief that Nero at his utmost was but a hobbledehoy of thirty, and that the town bull is by ordinary an infant of seven or eight; and one prefers to be thought of as more mature than all that comes to.

*   *

*

In these reflections, my dear Grace, I have strayed a bit widely from your letter. I now return to it and to you, asking that you may not resent my regarding you for an instant as a type rather than as an individual person. When you first began to write to me as a type, just after the World War, I had, I confess, my unworthy suspicions. It seemed to me that in logic you must be either a practical joker or a professional daughter of joy, if not a prospective black-mailer. In logic, you still must be: but I do not think you have much concern with logic. For by-and-by you began to write from addresses where I could verify you; and upon two occasions I managed also to see you without your knowing.

It was thus a profound shock to my faith in human nature to find you, my child, no impostor, but, in five instances at least, precisely what you had represented yourself. You were a person of good repute, not notable for excursions into excessive humor; you were young and pretty. (I preferred you upon the whole the time you had ashen blond hair, but as a brunette also did you satisfy the gaze of your unnoted appraiser prodigally.) In three instances you were self-supporting, twice you were well-to-do and lived idly at your parents' expense; but always you were known to have literary aspirations. You were enamored, in fine, with literature (or at least with the notion of seeing your own writings in print and of mingling with the topmost literati), and you were enamored too with what I have no doubt you described to yourself as freedom to live your own life: for now that the stale swamps of bourgeois morality were being drained, and the results written up handsomely in *The American Mercury* and in all the radical weeklies, a new era had made it possible for youth to pursue its ideals with a noble frankness which &c., &c.

Well, and so to-day, in the light of experience, I can believe that you are quite sincere in the naïve offer of your person, and that you really do intend through copulation with me both to confirm your dedication to letters and to develop your literary powers. One may not pretend to follow your logic: I remark only that it is tolerably familiar. I remark also that, perhaps without your clearly knowing this much as yet, you plan to commandeer by-and-by my assistance in getting your novels published.

I can thus reply to your entire letter with one word. That word is Scat! I speak it firmly but without anger. I do not resent being regarded as a means toward your desired ends, or being made a medicine to be taken for your literary welfare: I do not even resent being cast in the ungracious rôle of Hippolytus, a part which none plays to applause. Instead, with a large and mildly wistful sympathy, I consider that your main need of me is as a help to getting whatsoever you may write into print. I remember youth and what very odd notions youth can entertain as to the customs and the importance of a literary career. I remember (or, rather, I most resolutely decline to remember) the delusions about literature which I too cherished at twenty. The mere thought of them causes my cheeks to incarnadine; and in the hot glow of that blush my heart softens like melting wax. I say Scat! yet again, but I speak the word almost tenderly.

For a literary person, I am, let me protest, fairly modest: and common-sense does not urge me to believe that with quite all these indicated adorings you can regard a gray wordmonger whom you have never seen. I am sure, in any case (after some sad consultation with a mirror) that upon our meeting, your recovery would be so expeditious as to pain both of us.

For myself, I confess, I do not at all like the conveyance in which every aging male artist goes about earth. And I pause here to remark that I have considered many such makeshifts outside my own looking glass. Each reminded me of a shabby and time-battered coach, with all the curtains down; and when the lone occupant peeped out, he seemed to me to wear a mask. It was almost always a comic mask, not frozen in uproarious laughter but set forever in a half-contemptuous and half-placating snigger. If there be any mobile human face behind that mask its owner has long ago forgotten what it is like, I reflect in those darker moments when the month's bills have proved larger than I expected, or when Christmas approaches. I concede that this mask is but a sort of armor which the too sensitive artist needs badly in a world of practical persons of whom he is, at heart, I rather think, afraid; he does well to wear it, I know: yet I observe without deep elation the fact that every talented male writer some while before he becomes successful has learned to peep out at life from behind one or another mask.

From this much of irrelevant consideration I deflect to admit that the bargain which I imagine you to have in mind, at the very bottom of your mind, under all the bright gauds of romantic nonsense and under youth's normal desire for new experience, is neither out of reason nor unknown. It occurs to me that, without any special concealment, a fair number of such masked male writers have thus sponsored, and have launched in the bright stream of current letters, their personable young female associates, as a due acknowledgment for personal favors received. Indeed I myself, I reflect,—and then decide not to finish the sentence. But I check off on my ten finger-tips a dizain of ladies who have thus got into literature at night, and who have thrived there, some of them in quite prominent stations: and I could convict at least another ten upon strong circumstantial evidence. I admit all this: and I repeat, nevertheless, I repeat firmly, Scat!

*   *

*

For I am not, you see, really a member of the topmost literary circles. I encounter the élite, I grant you, every now and then; and we get on well enough, with a mutual civility which at all times stays removed, by a great many degrees, from intimacy. About their reactions I cannot say: but I profoundly enjoy an occasional meeting with our leading literati, especially with those pre-eminent geniuses who go to publishers' teas and are mentioned by columnists.

I like the élite, just as I like the talking pictures, as good for a two hours' diversion, provided always that you do not attend this form of entertainment too frequently or stay overtime. If I lived in a moving picture theatre, with the performance incessantly in progress, I suspect I would tire of it. If I lived in the best literary circles, and so had forever to remember just who was cohabiting with whom this week, and about precisely what bit of backbiting who was at feud with whom this week, and which was the correct book to sneer at this week, I believe that the involved mental strain, the absolute need to keep up-to-date in all these intellectual requirements, would prevent me also from getting any actual writing done this week.

In brief, I have not exactly the entrée, my dear child, and I could not, without taking entirely too much trouble, smuggle you into these glittering circles, and thus introduce you, as it were, to the court life of Bohemia. And that, I imagine, is what you have set your heart on. I enclose therefore the addresses of three well-known writers, and of two eminent critics, who could, and who from what I know of them will (if but your aspect be truly engaging), serve all your desires. I except in some degree the first-named writer, who has no longer any physical need for women beyond a little genial fumbling, but who keeps up appearances nobly by retaining always at least a pair of them in nominal employment. Nor will the owner of the name checked in violet ink, I am afraid, use you normally; it is possible that you husband a prejudice against the exotic here: to the other side, he can (if but his other lectual engagements permit) get you both published and reviewed handsomely, and a modest compliance may seem to you no stiff price for a career.

But for myself I observe, *Parce, precor!* The reign of my own special good Cynara seems nowadays as remote as the reign of Semiramis. I cry farewell to Venus Pandemos. I desire the imperious mother of light Loves to guide no more with silken reins a steed with whose mouth the dentist is over-familiar, a steed now by no means so near as I could wish to ten lustres in age. I bid Venus instead to hasten to the house of Maximus, or at least of Major; and to favor everybody concerned by taking you along with her.

* *

*

Yet I relinquish you in this fashion, my dear Grace, a trifle unwillingly. I am tempted, on the one hand, to admonish. I could write you much grave advice, not precisely as to the importance of virtuous conduct, of a proper respect for your pastor, or of the integrity of any special membrane, but as to the odd fact that every woman writer whom I have known appeared a restless and dissatisfied creature, forever clamorous because her art was not appreciated at its full worth. Male writers are no less exigent at bottom, I daresay, but they do fret less audibly, and with much longer pauses for boasting. Women writers, in brief, are not happy, and their writing does not content them: I state the fact without comment, because of my profound ignorance as to what may be either the true explanation or the fit moral. And I do not, not for one instant, urge you to profit by this fact, because I know very well that twenty can never profit by anything except experience, and I think too that experience is a tonic which kills rather more of mankind than it fortifies.

I am tempted, on the other hand, on the sinister hand, to gather me roses while yet I may, or, if roses seem a whit out of season in the middle fifties, at least to pluck the fair and late-flowering cosmos of autumn, before entirely giving over all floral appreciation. It would be easy and far less impolite, it would be more in accord with the dictates of Southern chivalry, I reflect, to say Come! After that I could affect quite plausibly, I believe, a semi-paternal interest in your welfare, for, heaven knows, I have seen the thing done often enough.

And besides, my reason tells me: It is well, it is wholly equitable, that Merlin should have his Vivien—as Louis Quinze his Du Barry, as David his Abishag—to divert the late afternoon of life with her light and gracious trickeries; to delude his cooling vigor, docilely, with sweet cheats which he does not much more than half see through; and thus to beguile the old lecher in part, and at all and any event to entertain him consumedly. Somebody will be having such enterprising young women very soon, in any case, says my reason yet further: it is not in the least as though they displayed any vocation for the nunnery. Unplucked as yet, they ripen bedward, they ripen apace, they ripen with fond lusciousness.

Then my conscience, after wincing a little at

the word "lecher," my conscience too joins in, observing sedately: In fact, if the girl really does possess any literary talent, it is almost your bounden duty to help, or at any rate to have a look at her— I do not mean, that is, of course (says my conscience, hastily), any nonsense about a mole or anything of the sort. I mean that you might be of some much needed help to the girl after you had once seen her and had a completely unprejudiced look at her writing. The mole can wait until afterward.

So do I listen to both my reason and my conscience with an impatience to which the poor things have become more or less accustomed by this time. Then I return to my formula. And I say, yet once again, Scat!

THE EIGHTH LETTER

✻　　✻

✻

MIRROR AND PIGEONS

My dear Sir:

It was wholly a pleasure to
receive your letter, and I am very
grateful for the kindly things you
say therein.   I am afraid, even so,
I can but repeat what I have said in
another place: that each of my books
is narrated from a definite point of
view, and that matters not ever made
clear to my protagonist must be left
unexplained, necessarily.

I am sorry -- and I stay

Yours faithfully,

Branch Cabell

31 September 1932

MIRROR AND PIGEONS

*   *

*

You, *sir*, *have written me a wholly charming* letter, the point of which, as you explain toward the end of the seventh page, is to ask about an odd alliance between white pigeons and a small mirror (three inches square, to be precise) which appears time and again in so many of my books. The envelope of your letter displays two English stamps, and it comes, I observe, from a village in Berkshire which I well remember as one of the former homes of the Branch family: though indeed very much the same letter has come to me before this morning, bearing hundreds of other postmarks.

The reader who wants to know what this or that passage "means" is rather constantly with me when I open the morning's mail. He requests omniscience and will be satisfied with nothing less, finding always in those eighteen volumes which compose the Biography of the life of Manuel an enigma or two for me to unravel by return post. He implores (for example) a more particular account of the murder of Scott Musgrave: and anagrams he desiderates of the one or the other proper name. He assumes every name I mention to be an anagram. As an unfledged bird cries out from its nest, tirelessly, even so does he inquire from his half sheet of paper, Who was Horvendile? He demands of me, What manner of talisman, formed with what shaping, did Jurgen show to the Brown Man? He desires to know of what nature were those beings whom Dom Manuel encountered outside the Window of Ageus? He interrogates if Maya should be regarded as Mother Eve, yet alive, in at least the nineteenth century? And he asks if the famed Sigil of Scoteia were not engraved with characters (it may be, of Dirghic origin) which when read upside down still harbor significance?

About such quite negligible riddles do my correspondents concern themselves. Such questions and some scores of allied questions have been addressed to me off and on, now for twelve years, to my postman's wearying. Yet these questions vary somewhat, they arrive intermittently, and in a shifting volume, where one question alone does not vary, nor ever leave me unmolested for a reasonable breathing spell. I would count it a strange week which did not produce your letter, my dear sir, requesting that I explain my perpetual dealings with white pigeons and a small mirror.

To speak frankly, this is a matter which I have never made clear to anyone before to-day. This has been, until to-day, the secret which for me has unified the perpetuated life of Manuel in its innumerable manifestations; the secret which lay glowing at the inmost heart of my many books unseen by any beholder (I believe) save only me; the secret from which I drew a smug sense of superiority so long as I alone, to all seeming, still knew of its simplicity, its strength, its truth, and its splendor. I have preferred in consequence (and, no doubt, selfishly) to keep this little matter of the mirror and the pigeons a secret known only to me.

But yours is an irresistible letter, in that you

extol my literary achievements at appropriate
length (in a wholly legible handwriting, too),
and express your wonder that my books are not
appreciated more widely by the literati of England. With such bait you may entrap the gratitude of any author known to me, so potent is
the insatiable vanity of our fretting tribe, and to
such bait I respond, smirking and garrulous. Yet
before answering your question I really must
pause to remark that, for an American, I have
been treated with fair indulgence, I believe, by
the reviewers indigenous to your island. I have
fared a deal better than do most of my nation
under their hortatory attention, and I have
amassed indeed, during the last twelve years, a
full half-dozen quite civil press cuttings to attest
this fact.

Of all these, let me observe, the most frequently read by me remains a longish review
which begins, "Although Mr. Cabell is an American writer, his books are not books to be de-
spised." Thereafter every comment is favorable,
and in a British fashion almost enthusiastic, but
the rest of the notice is not to my immediate
purpose. I delight only in the initial sentence,

which embodies so perfectly the Englishman's
attempt, in all circumstances, howsoever pro-
vocative, to be affable to an American.

*   *

*

To return now to that matter of the mirror
and the pigeons, the postmark of your letter re-
calls to me very pleasantly those weeks which I
once devoted, within six miles of your present
home, to persuading the sexton of St. Helen's
Church at Abingdon to unlock a corner cupboard. This cupboard contained parish records
relative to the Branch family, of which I was
then compiling a history; and these records were
admittedly open to the public. But for an American gentleman, sir, to be wishful to see them, I
gathered from their polite, fluttered, but firm
custodian, raised points not satisfyingly covered
by canonical precedent. Nor did the offering and
the glib reception of a tip get us beyond the
general statement that never in his time at least,
sir, had any American gentleman—! I could in-

fer at best from the sexton's slightly softened manner that just possibly, at some remote period, well prior to the Norman Conquest, one other inexplicable American had preceded me in barbaric presumptuousness. In any case, it developed, I could write to the vicar.

I erred. I admit that I erred. I offered to walk over to the vicar's near-by home and to explain to him my simple need to have a cupboard door unlocked. For one chilling instant it was quite as though I had offered to set fire to the church. Then I was pitied. I was even humored. The fact was again made clear to me, in the tones of one addressing a fractious and unusually dull-witted child, that I could write to the vicar.

It was my allotted part to cross no church-yard, babbling irresponsibly of high matters. It was my part, instead, through the more august channels of formal correspondence (after duly confessing my real name, and profession, and home address), to break the news to the vicar of St. Helen's Church, as tactfully as could be managed, that I wished to lay American eyes on the parish register dating from 1538 and the churchwardens' accounts beginning with the

year 1555. The dates were essential. After his
to-be-hoped-for rally, the vicar of St. Helen's, I
gleaned (in the while that I reminded myself
this was Abingdon, and not Titipu) would in
proper form consult with himself, in his superior
capacity as rector of St. Nicholas' Church, about
this (it was not hidden from me) distressing
state of affairs. It was conceivable, if not likely,
at least conceivable, that as vicar Dr. Maitland
might request, and as rector accord, a benison on
my prying curiosity. Then if the bishop approved, sir (out of, I gathered, a bishop's wide
experience of human depravity, especially as it
flourished in America), the matter might, it was
just possible, be condoned.

I am afraid, though, that as a rector Herbert
T. Maitland, D. D., was more cautious in judgment than as a vicar he was eloquent in pleading
my case, or perhaps the Bishop of Oxford had
to refer the imbroglio to the Archbishop of
Canterbury, inasmuch as a fortnight passed by
before the sexton of St. Helen's had all the
needed permits which would enable him to take
the key out of his pocket and to unlock the corner cupboard in the vestry room. He sat by me

then while I consulted the parish records; and I had the feeling, during my meek transcription of my remote relatives' births and marriages and deaths, that he was fully armed, with at least two pistols, and ready for any possible nonsense on my part.

*   *

*

In these fond reflections, sir (begotten inevitably by your postmark), I may seem to have wandered some little way from the secret of the mirror and the pigeons. But the case is otherwise: and to that theme I approach steadily. It is in a connection with this very theme that my thoughts now turn to yet further conflicts with British custom in that far-away time when I was getting together the material for a small book about the Branch family.

I think, for example, of my forlorn endeavors, while on this same quest, to procure a reader's ticket at the British Museum. I think of all those partially or resplendently bald-headed, those precise, and those pince-nez'd Under Librarians (each one of them remarkably like a brand-new and glossy wax figure, but, if anything, rather more animated than a wax figure) who made the fact plain that an unidentified American might quite as rationally have asked for the Elgin Marbles or the Portland Vase. I think of how repeatedly I was allowed to state, in writing, my name, profession, address, and purpose, and questioned as to the range of my acquaintanceship among house-holders in London. It is not possible, I then learned, to convince an Englishman that anybody exists who does not know a great many persons in London: the British mind simply does not grasp the idea. And I think of the final reluctant compromise (reached, I have no doubt, at a special meeting of the Board of Trustees, after a consultation with Scotland Yard) that my strange desire might, just conceivably, be considered with more or less seriousness after it had been officially endorsed, at 123 Victoria Street, S. W., by the American Ambassador.

I think too of how at the Embassy I encountered a marked reluctance (with which, at bottom, I sympathized) to make an international affair out of my reader's ticket. Passports were not obligatory in those days; and I had none: and nobody had ever heard of me at the Embassy, nor could the testimony of either *Who's Who* or of *Who's Who in America* be regarded as acceptable evidence of my actual existence. All the attachés were quite frank about that. Nor did I find that the interest of any attaché in historical research work was morbid. And when I eventually got my reader's ticket (which in the irrational outcome did come to pass) it was only through pure accident, in accord with no rule made and provided by the American Embassy or the British Museum.

I think also, I think with squirms and blushes, of how in Somerset House I paid properly enough my shilling to see the sixteenth century will of one of my forebears in which I was interested; and of how, when this will was laid before me, I took out a pencil so that I might make an abstract. I do not recall, at this late date, just how many clerks and head clerks and subclerks, guards, office boys, policemen, stenographers, and porters, sprang into action, uproarious at the sight of that two-inch pencil. I am merely sure that in my country we lynch with less noisiness, and that had I produced a dynamite bomb no more officials could have leapt about me with such markedly un-British volubility. In fact, I have never since then been able to believe that an Englishman is really phlegmatic. I learned at all events that at the Probate Registry in Somerset House one paid to look at this or the other will, hiring but a visual indulgence; and that to attempt a copy of any public record deposited there, was a crime punishable with hanging, castration, disembowelment, and quartering of the offender's body, under a statute enacted, I believe, by either Hengist or Horsa.

In the upshot, however, I was allowed to state, in writing, my name, profession, address, and purpose, and (after some little cross-examination relative to the house-holders of London) to procure official copies of all the wills I required, at eight pence the folio page. I received also (to my final and complete confusion) something like an apology. It developed that I had been in the right all along. I was right, not because the public records in the Probate Registry were preserved there for the benefit of the public, but because the will at which I was looking when I took out my pencil was dated prior to 1700. The remote dating of this will alone, it developed, had saved my life, and viscera, and other appurtenances.

You must bear with me, my dear sir. I am not really straying from my theme when I hark back to these trivial-seeming misadventures of a foreigner at loose ends in a land whose customs and faiths are strange to him. I believe, you see, that, as some profound philosopher or another has stated, "life is like that." I find that every man lives, and eventually dies, among an infinity of unexplained restraints and unexplained formulas. I, for example, I still do not understand why the sexton of St. Helen's could not unlock his cupboard without waiting to involve two parishes and one see (and, for all I know, an archbishop) of the Church of England. It is a mystery which still preys on my mind now and then when I lie awake at night. I do not understand why my reader's ticket could not be granted, to a self-evidently harmless person, as an aid to consulting the books in the British Museum Library, rather than as a reward for knowing a well-to-do woman who lived in Berkeley Square. Nor do I understand how any one being, far less a mob, can be incited to madness by the sight of a pencil, and then pacified by a mention of 1700. I know only that there was a reason, not ever revealed to me, for each of these British mysteries. So I shrug and pass on.

* *

*

Well, and in just this way lives the protagonist of each of my books. Each lives, during his travel in lands unfamiliar to him (precisely as you and I live, my dear sir, throughout the jogtrot of our daily vocation), in a welter of un-explained matters, of half-glimpsed human con-cernments with which he himself is not concerned, in so far as he knows, and of ever-present uncomprehended forces and affairs and plans, of which he divines the existence without fathoming their nature. I can but tell the reader what this protagonist heard or saw, or in other wise perceived and endured. Manuel no more understood Suskind than did I my sexton; how Kennaston came by the Sigil of Scoteia remained to Kennaston always as much an irrationality as to me remains the provenance of my reader's ticket at the British Museum; and to Jurgen the behavior of the Brown Man after seeing a talisman appeared quite as unaccountable as I found the behavior of the employees of Somerset House when I showed them a pencil.

It is so with the secret of the mirror and the pigeons. Since no one of my protagonists entirely fathomed this secret, there was no need, and I lacked any plausible occasion, to explain this matter to the reader. I can see no hurt, though, nowadays, in my making clear to you, in a less formal fashion, and upon but one condition, this by-end of old magic.

What man discovered it, or what being first revealed it to man, I do not know. Like most true magic, as distinguished from hocus-pocus, it is older than any recorded history, it is older than what we describe as "science." Nor is it at any real enmity with science, no matter how whole-heartedly the latest phases of immortal science may appear to assail it.

I mean of course that present-day science which, being of a practical turn, dismisses magic as an illusion and restricts itself to more sturdy novelties, such as airplanes and bacteria and evolution. I mean that science which accepts the aviation of Colonel Lindbergh, but denies the aviation of Simon Magus. I mean that wholly long-headed and matter-of-fact science which scoffs at any rumored manifestations of "the occult" in the same moment that it pronounces such an everyday affair as a cold in the head to be caused by unknown agents; and which gets, somehow, out of its conviction that millions of monkeys were transformed into men, a proof that no one learned lady could be transformed into a cat. I mean, in brief, a remarkably transitory concatenation of faiths and teachings, all which are just now in excellent standing, and the most of which will by-and-by consort with the science of Sir John Mandeville, the science of Albertus Magnus, the science of the Elder Pliny, the science of Aristotle, and the science of Moses. For, let it be repeated, science is immortal, and like most other immortals, science is much given to metamorphoses.

The secret of the mirror and the pigeons is based upon certain facts, upon three facts, before naming which I must pause to admit that the facts of magic are, to be sure, not the same as the facts of science. For magic remains virtually stable, in a world wherein (as you have no doubt observed, my dear sir) the known truths of science vary perpetually. And to say that, is, of course, not to disparage science. Few blessings can long remain unaltered. Thus women vary perpetually, and so keep the world handsomely provided with gossip and milliners and lyric poetry. The weather varies from hour to hour; and if it failed to vary, we would all starve. Did a thermometer not vary, of what earthly good would it be? Well, and just so may the facts of science also vary, just as beneficently, within their own field of diurnal usefulness.

*　　　*

*

For, to return now to the mystery of the mirror and the pigeons, man, as I and a great many other people have pointed out, fares among ever-present mysteries. These necessarily perturb him.

But science rationalizes all, by explaining everything, so that no educated person need any longer live in apprehension of the unknown. Science has thus soothed us. It has brought to us, at different times, the glad news that vaccination warded off smallpox, and that to wear an amethyst prevented drunkenness; that each man was a modified monkey, and that premature childbirth was incited by the mother's stepping upon, or perhaps over, a fern leaf; that the aurora borealis was due to positively charged corpuscles of helium, and that Earth was a large disk with a river running around its edges. It has found out the texture of the rainbow, the area of Costa Rica, the origin of the moon, the ninety-nine secret names of God, and the uses of gasoline. It has proved to us that an elephant has no joints, and that mosquitoes transmit yellow fever, and that suture of the alar bone is peculiar to Japanese crania, and that to eat the brains of a camel will cure epilepsy. It has plugged our teeth to prevent decay, and then pulled them out to prevent focal infection. It has discovered vitamins, dissected the genitals of the male grasshopper, and revealed the ways of the basilisk.

To know, beyond any question, the true facts about these matters has been an unfailing comfort to mankind, in that the world and his wife no longer lived among ever-present mysteries. Science has made all clear, since the days of Nimrod. It has afforded to mankind that succor, that consolation, and that perennial inspiriting, which but too many unreflective people consider to be equally the fruitage of religion.

I am afraid, as a communicant of the Protestant Episcopal Church, that religion has never been quite so potent as science has always been to serve every cultured person who lives as yet, under a death sentence, as a tranquillizing narcotic. Religion can offer but a removed prospect, a hope, of escaping from the unexplained restrictions and the ever-present perils of our transient life upon earth, by-and-by, into more luxurious and more stable surroundings. But science goes straight to the root of our trouble: it removes, or it at worst ameliorates, all menaces forthwith,

Mirror and Pigeons

by explaining them. It explains the restrictions, it explains the perils, it explains everything, in decisive terms, and it so rids man of his chief terror, his dread of the unknown.

I need hardly point out that the truthfulness of these explanations is an irrelevant matter. The Phœnician ship-captain sailed intrepidly about an Earth which he knew to be a large disk with an uncrossable river forever circling its edges, so that he could not possibly fall off: his ocean stream was an affair accounted for, set down plainly on an up-to-date, scientific map, with no improbable nonsense about it nor any least element of the surprising. He knew just as well and just as firmly what a prosaic business engaged his working hours as may the captain of any modern ocean liner. The latter believes, to be sure, that, safely held on by the force of gravity, he steams about the exterior of an oblate spheroid, having a diameter of 7918 miles and a mean daily motion of slightly over 3548 miles, but the difference here is a mere matter of opinion. The point is that both skippers should be assured as to their whereabouts and as to exactly what they are doing, and in both instances their needs have been attended to by contemporaneous science.

No, it is the main function of science, as it is of religion, to create faith. And science possesses the large advantage that, where religion has to be explicit in its revealings, science need not tender us any such direct information in order to work its thaumaturgy. When no great while ago, for example, Prof. Dr. Albert Einstein explained the entire cosmos, and we heard there were but a dozen living persons who could understand his explanation, we all felt none the less the vast consolation of science. It was most reassuring to know at least that the cosmos had been found out and detected in all its doings, so that under the cold vigilance of twenty-six stern scientific eyes the cosmos would have to be more careful for the future. We all felt, I am sure, that the cosmos at any rate had been disposed of, and the weight of it was off our minds.

So does science continue to rid us of the un-known, in its old beneficent fashion, just as when that first great scientist, Moses, accounted rather more plainly for the cosmos, as a six-day job with all the necessary imperfections of such hurried work. So has science always begotten faith and understanding, with some slight assistance from human logic. It is for this reason, above all other reasons, that no one of us ought ungratefully to disparage science, and that I have been at pains to disavow any such intention before I explain at length the secret of the mirror and the pigeons.

Yet in return for communicating this secret I shall ask, I repeat, in this regrettably self-seeking world, one little favor. You live within a half-hour's jaunt of Abingdon. It should not deeply inconvenience you, who know the lay of pleasant Berkshire, to find out what rules do actually apply to the opening of that cupboard (to the south side of the building, on the same side as Holy Cross aisle, and facing a picture of Christ bearing His Cross) in the snug vestry room of St. Helen's Church? to what sesame move the hinges of that cupboard? and with what rites, what exsufflations, or what cantraps (apart, of course, from crude tips) should I have approached that cupboard's sanctity and sexton in due form? It does not appear plausible that in no circumstances could a cupboard door be unclosed within less than a fortnight, and then only after a clergyman had weighed gravely his own recommendations to himself concerning that cupboard, with his Grace the Lord Bishop of Oxford officiating as the referee in all matters pertaining to that cupboard. I feel that, Aladdin-like, I evoked strange British djinns, unknowing. I feel, I still feel, perturbed about it.

In brief, nor science nor religion nor magic may quite explain the ways of you English to an American; and this matter has long puzzled me, now for some twenty years. So do you solve, if it be permitted, this secret for me, and by return post I will forward you the secret of the mirror and the pigeons.

THE NINTH LETTER

* *

*

LITURGY IN DARKNESS

3201 MONUMENT AVENUE
RICHMOND, VIRGINIA

My dear Sir:

        It was wholly a pleasure to
receive your letter, and your scheme
sounds both interesting and alluring.
I only wish it were possible for me
to take part in a symposium of so
great value and importance; but by
ill luck I now have so much overdue
work in hand that every moment of my
time is pre-engaged for months yet
to come.

        I am sorry -- for both our
sakes,-- and I stay

                        Yours faithfully,

                        Branch Cabell

31 September 1932

LITURGY IN DARKNESS

*   *

*

$\mathcal{T}$*he postman has brought me letters from but* three of your tribe to-day, my dear sir, as I observe with relief. The first of you, I find, is making a study of sundry "outstanding personalities" from the standpoint of, "To what extent did your early training and family background contribute to your personal success?" This problem is to be disposed of by the victim's answering ten questions, of which each is divided into some half-dozen sub-sections, questions of a highly ramified, of an exhaustive, and here and there of a delicate nature, questions which (I estimate roughly) I might dispose of in rather less than a month's steady work. The second of you is compiling a book of "personal messages of cheer and comfort" to be distributed among the inmates of tuberculosis hospitals; and I among others am being asked to sustain the moribund in optimism and hilarity. And you, sir, are preparing a "symposium upon religion," for which you desire my "personal views, theories, or beliefs, concerning religion, together with the reasons for these views, whether they be philosophical, scientific, or theological."

I may not pretend to understand you immoderate persons who thus pester authors to take part in "symposiums." Upon purely sordid grounds, I, who am of Scots descent, marvel that you should expect authors to drop whatever work they may have in hand and to combine gratis to write for you your book, your pamphlet, or your magazine article. From the standpoint of mere rationality, I have never found that any such "symposium," when once it was completed and set forth in print, displayed any detectable reason to justify its existence. It publicates, for the most part, only the ostensible views of quite unimportant persons as to topics about which they know nothing in particular; and one honestly does wonder why the hodgepodge was electrotyped.

Not every practising author (I would whisper

to you, sir, in close confidence) is omniscient. It follows that when a writer is called upon off-hand to speak of socialism, his favorite recipe, the future of literature, Christmas, the immortality of the soul, alcohol, his ideal woman, the younger generation, his most awkward moment, the best books of the year, the talking pictures, divorce, censorship, the capitalistic régime, and how he intends to vote at the next election—all which may very easily happen to an unwary writer upon any morning in his life—not every one of his dicta can be of universal interest and of perdurable worth. Quite a number of them in fact will be damned silly. And I think that to every writer who does not abstain absolutely from such "symposiums" one may apply just the same description.

I do not attempt humor. Did these "symposiums" aim but at frivolous topics there would be in them no great harm. My complaint is that they don't. My complaint is, for example, that they enable a chuckle-headed altruist to draw on me for "a personal message of cheer and comfort" for hospitalfuls of men and women dying of consumption. It is of course a draft very far beyond my mental funds: I myself have come reasonably near to dying upon several occasions, and upon none of them could I contrive to make even myself feel cheery and comfortable. Death did not, somehow, appeal to me as a brisk pleasure jaunt; I was wholly willing to postpone it; and the nearlier it approached, the more fretfully did I regard it, with the irrational but strong distaste which I had hitherto reserved for golf and horseback exercise. It might suit other people well enough, if they cared for that sort of thing, I felt, but not me. I wanted not to die, not for the present, anyhow. I did not want, not immediately, to be an angel and with the angels stand. I wanted a corps of physicians at my bedside and all the better-thought-of drugs in extra large quantities.

Who, then, am I to recommend the King of Terrors as an uncommonly good fellow when you come really to know him? I do not know anything about death save that all his ways, in so far as I have witnessed them, are tyrannous and unclean and terrible.

And yet, you see, I feel that after all one might pocket both common-sense and one's awkward memories philanthropically. I feel that one could perhaps contrive some sort of opiate claptrap which might, just possibly, hoodwink a few of the less intelligent consumptives into a half-belief which would a little ease their going out of this world. And I know that for me to do this for even one person would seem (to me, at all events) a far more laudable performance than to cling selfishly to mere mental integrity. And I know too that I am so constituted I cannot contrive this claptrap. So the sole fruitage of the matter is that I come to abhor the chuckle-headed altruist who has made me feel bitterly uncomfortable. After that I do not drop his letter hastily into the waste-paper basket, but instead I scrouge it down with ferocity.

*   *

*

To your letter, however, I may reply with comparative calm. I need but tell you I am a communicant of the Protestant Episcopal Church of America. I accept its creeds (both of them; and including of course the Thirty-Nine Articles) as being, in so far as I can understand their statements, quite possibly true. The remaining and the major portions of the tenets of my church I regard as indisputable, if but because they convey to me no earthly meaning, and nobody can dispute the incomprehensible. You cannot, for example, rationally deny that you believe in the Holy Ghost until somebody has provided you with some faint notion of the Holy Ghost. Pending that, I find no great difficulty in accepting His existence, very much as I accept the existence of the Amir of Afghanistan, without forming any mental concept of either.

All these tentative acceptances and these meek desires to avoid argument, I should further explain, I attest in due form. I attest them by attending divine worship, if not regularly at eleven o'clock on each Sunday morning, at least at eight o'clock on each Maundy Thursday. I am partial, if but comparatively partial, to the service set for that evening, as it is conducted at the small country church which my wife frequents, and which I attend at any rate once a year, for, if the reflections which this service arouses are not, to my finding, entirely of a religious nature, yet do they retain their interest.

*   *

*

When we enter, the church is wholly dark save for the two lights on the altar. The congregation is assembled, I know, but all sit perfectly quiet and all stay unseen in the hushed gloom. I can but guess that the building is partly filled with seated rows of my fellow creatures: them also I must accept as yet on faith. We reach our invisible pew, guided by some sort of instinct; and I duly bow down my forehead so that it touches the back of the pew in front of us. I remain thus postured for a suitable while, without any notion of what else one is expected to do during this initial ceremony of church attendance.

I imagine that my wife beside me is praying. It seems rather tactless, to be asking for personal favors in the very first instant you enter the church. It occurs to me that I could approximately fill in the interval wherein etiquette keeps my head depressed if I recited to myself the multiplication tables from "Once one is one" to about "Twice six is twelve." I abstain from doing so. I raise my head, allowing an extra second or two for good measure, after I notice that my wife has raised her head.

Now the church bell not far above us begins to ring. Its ringing is irregular and harsh and menacing. It is meant, I know, as an invitation, or at utmost as a summons, to divine worship; but it sounds far more like a threat, a metallic, blustering, almost maudlin threat, bellowed at random through the spring night. I can now see more clearly. I can see that the front pews to my left, reserved for the well-to-do communicants, are all vacant. I can see that the red strip of carpet in the church aisle appears, in this imperfect and oblique lighting, to be higher and more immediate to the eye. It is as though I were sitting down on this carpet and it were not more than two feet away from my eyes. I think about my last trip to the oculist's. I remember that in his waiting-room he has a fine color print of Old Blandford Church and a desirable engraving of

Liturgy in Darkness

The Surrender at Yorktown. I remember the droll painting at Versailles in which this surrender is worked over into an exclusively French victory.

An opening door creaks, like a jeer. The rector appears vaguely in the gloom to the right of the altar. I observe that the stole about his neck is obscurely red—or perhaps it is purple. There is some rule, I believe, as to his wearing differently colored stoles at the various church seasons. He hesitates. He has forgotten something needed for the evening's rite. He fetches it (I cannot see what) from that yet more profound darkness which enshrouds, I know, the baptismal font. This leads me to recollect that there are five liturgical colors, because the purplish or violet stole is worn at baptisms. He must have on the red one. He approaches the altar, and the two lights set there make him now wholly visible. He kneels, with his back to us, beneath the two tables of the Decalogue which rise dimly beyond the white altar. Only the fourth, the ninth and the tenth commandment are illuminated, at the bottom of the stone-gray tablets, as if these three requirements alone remained in force.

Special Delivery

We watch the kneeling man without any of us moving. I reflect that my hair also is thin at the back. But then he is older than I am. When we went to school together he was a little taller than I. A great many of the boys with whom we went to school have been dead for a long while. When I am dead it is this man, in all probability, who will drop earth on my coffin. He stands up, and he faces us, with a strange grave look, which is somewhere between compassion and ecstasy. He speaks.

*   *

*

So does the service begin, and continue, in darkness. The congregation cannot see to read the proper responses; and take refuge in non-committal mumblings. The rector too errs now and then, and corrects himself, as he reads aloud in his little island of faint lighting. All seems improvised and uncertain. All of us seem to be groping in the dark, groping toward an unseen and guessed-at power which we can but hope to be kindly, and which we do not know, not with any certainty, how to invoke nor how to placate. My right foot threatens to "go to sleep" and prickles everywhere with small tinglings. I bear down hard upon it, and I wriggle its toes hurriedly, for I know the communion service is about to begin.

It does. My wife and I go forward to our usual places, well to the right of the chancel rail, where one may kneel without any sense of exposing to the congregation an irreverent rump and the soles of one's shoes. We kneel there, with extended cupped hands. My foot is not really asleep after all. The color of the stole turns out to be crimson.

I take part, I reflect, in the supreme mystery of our faith. I could wish that I responded to it more deeply. The sacred bread seems hard and stale in my mouth. I recollect Bulwer Lytton's *Harold*, and how Earl Godwin choked and fell, "sudden and heavy, smitten by the stroke of apoplexy," when he attempted to swallow a crumb of such blessed bread, in an insufficiently religious state of mind. I moisten my own bit of bread very thoroughly with saliva, before attempting to swallow it; and to my relief, it goes down easily enough. I survive the ordeal by *corsnaed*. I thought it would go down, of course, but you can never be certain. I wonder if I shall ever get around again to reading Bulwer Lytton? Once he seemed majestic, witty, and all-glorious: now, like this bread, no doubt, there would be an undeniable flavor of staleness.

The wine appears slightly sour; and I, who have lately eaten a largish supper, reflect, as I swallow this wine on top of it, that I tend nowadays to acidity of the stomach. This wine will not help matters. I decide on a calcium carbonate tablet the very instant we are back home again. These reflections are not suited to the communion table. I am an elderly and responsible inheritor of the bright kingdom of heaven, who should at this moment be revolving the most profound and solemn thoughts. I hope that the beautiful old words now repeated to us, by my former school fellow, "Monk" Harrison, may be true. Our communion is over.

We return to our pew, largely by guesswork, treading through the dark choir stalls, where I feel my way cautiously with my feet, and leaving the middle aisle open for those who are now coming forward for the second communion. As we pass among our church fellows, on this warm spring evening, I encounter an aroma of Thursday arising from a congregation which lives by virtue of physical labor and bathes on Saturday. In our pew we again bow down our heads, for a full minute, to the back of the pew in front of us. I think dimly of reciting from "Twice seven is fourteen" up to "Three times twelve is thirty-six," but abstain from it.

*　　　*

*

At the altar I can still hear a continuing of the rector's half-confidential murmur in the while that he offers first one large silver goblet, then the other, to the kneeling semi-circle before him. As each goblet is restored to him he wipes its rim with a white cloth before handing it to the next communicant but one. He speaks steadily the beautiful old words, over and yet over again, without any pause or hurrying, and there is no sound but his lowered voice, and it is all rather nefarious seeming in this quiet dark place. I imagine that Mithras was worshipped thus in caves. I remember the Catacombs, where the first Christians held this service in darkness deep under the soil of Rome. I remember how my stepdaughter wrote (with a perfect summarizing of my own state of mind as a tourist), "There were so many things to look at in Rome that we decided we had better go to Florence." I think about the cavern upon Mount Elæon wherein was worshipped the Dark Goddess of Phigalia. I think about that gloomy subterranean oracle of Trophonius, to which the Bœotians were guided by a swarm of bees.

I observe that, somehow, we have attained more familiar ground, now that all of us are repeating the Lord's Prayer. The voices of the congregation are loud and confident and relieved now (as distinguished from those earlier, very vague responses), because everybody knows the Lord's Prayer. We recite it in the darkness with gusto. The words soar up fondly and proudly, and without any hesitancy. They have an honest, a really filial ring. It is as though we had found, somehow, some certainty, at last.

The rector leaves us. The door to the right of the altar creaks behind him, like a jeer. We hear him speak grave and inaudible words from the vestry room, dismissing us. We remain seated for a polite interval. Feet move just audibly, garments rustle, somebody coughs. We rise; and my wife begins to confer with Mrs. Johnston across the aisle about getting the church grounds cleaned up in time for Easter Sunday. Whether it would be cheaper to hire a man for the entire job, or to hire two men by the hour and keep an eye on them, is the prime affair moot.

Then the weather is commented on, without optimism: so too is the conduct of sundry members of the congregation who simply never do come to the Lenten services, and make it so discouraging for Mr. Harrison. You certainly would think that people with no real calls on them would try to set a better example. Both ladies are wholly at one as to the matter.

Half-visible grave persons shake hands with me in the gloom. They remark, with needless significance, that they are very glad to see me here. Dozens of handshaking persons thus remark solemnly, one by one, that they are very glad to see me here. It rather annoys me. When we reach the church door I shake hands with the rector, and I tell him, in the same earnest tones, that I am very glad to see him here. He does not like it either, I find. I can smoke now. I feel I have honored my Creator in due form, doing everything, in so far as I know, which is required of me by the Protestant Episcopal Church of America.

*   *

*

I record all this, my dear sir, in no spirit of flippancy. I record it with honesty, as a fair sample of my more formal dealings with the church of my faith. I elect, as I have said, to accept the tenets of this church as quite possibly true. I attend its services, whensoever my wife makes a point of it in her more actively disagreeable vein, and I get from its services just the sensations and the half-thoughts of which I have told you. And I am afraid that nobody can educe from the transaction my "personal views, theories, or beliefs." Certainly I cannot undertake the elaborate task. I would as lief try to hunt up for you some reasons of a "philosophical, scientific, or theological nature" which would seem to defend my part in this Maundy Thursday service from any rational standpoint.

To the other side, I am sure that the human mind is an imperfect and fallible instrument, not even intended (in so far as I know) to measure the origins and designs of our universe; so that to affirm man's reason cannot justify religion, may be but to restate the fact that with an inaccurate speedometer you cannot always, not to a nicety, calculate avoirdupois weights. Here Pascal had this large matter's root: it is the heart that feels God, not the reason. If your heart does but pump blood for you, undiscerningly, then you may go farther in this world than in the next. So I feel at least, without tactlessly adventuring into mental exercise. And I am sure this Maundy Thursday service, as it is thus conducted by the most prosaic and familiar people, has its own strange romantic beauty. I am sure these stumbled-through invocations in the darkness do wholly and most satisfyingly symbolize, not Christianity alone, but each and every religion.

From the deep dark we cry out to a wisdom very far above our blunders, to a strength above our feebleness, and to a kindliness above our spites, our lewdness, and our busy hatreds. To some power above us we cry out rather hopefully for compassion, upon the firm ground that creatures so pitiable deserve compassion: and we are certain that omniscience can hardly miss a point so plain to mere common-sense. Hearing, He must heed, in mere logic.

It may well be, of course, that there is no such power. Even more particularly in that case, if chance begot everything, if human life be but the nightmare of a dumb devil, and if we all be more fine and more noble than is our insensate creator, even more does it become the assured part of wisdom, I think, to believe in a wholly fine and a wholly noble Deity. Atheism in any such gray circumstances appears to me but the *non sequitur* that since all life is a passing disease, nobody ought to take opiates. For myself, when ill, I elect, as I have said, to accept all the better-thought-of drugs.

THE TENTH LETTER

*   *

*

ABOUT LOVELINESS REVISED

ABOUT LOVELINESS REVISED

*　　*

*

As I laid by your letter, madam, it seemed odd that your handwriting should be unchanged after all these years. Then I reflected that this same handwriting is the only link with our shared past, in that it is the one matter about you which to me stays recognizable. When I see you, and we talk together—a little distantly, a thought warily, and with some ever-present thin undercurrents of enmity and spite,—then I can perceive in you no trace of the mirthful and tender and, I daresay, rather rattlepate young person who once wrote to me in the handwriting which you still employ for your correspondence.

You are in these days an elderly woman with whom I feel not at all familiar. We meet civilly now and again; we make talk, exchanging stray bits of personal gossip and the tepidly indecent

jokes of middle-aged people; and upon the whole
we get on well enough. But between us lies the
grave of our love. We look at each other always
across that grave, with a discomfortable feeling
that if you and I had been more highly princi-
pled and more constant persons our love would
have endured. And in consequence, I think, we
can neither of us regard the other without some
distrust and irritation.

Your handwriting, that alone, remains unchanged. And the sentiments expressed thereby
I regard a thought ruefully. You have written, I
find, to ask that I autograph a book for the near
friend of a second cousin of a close acquaintance
of the pastor of the late partner in business of
the deceased husband of one of your former
schoolmates, or something of the kind. You are
asking, I reflect, one of those unwarrantable
promiscuous favors such as no sane writer likes
to accord, in the way of autographing his books
for a complete stranger; and you know it is a
plain imposition; and you know also that I resent
being pestered in this fashion; and moreover you
know that I, at any rate mildly, dislike the large

and autocratic matron you have become, and that I avoid her in so far as civility permits. And yet you haven't—confound you!—any least apparent doubt about my doing whatsover that aging and unlovable and unbrilliant and alienated person may ask. Nor have I, either.

I await the book. And I will break faith with my publishers and with my every most firm resolve, and I will write my name in your damned book, after a suitably untruthful and polite inscription, because it entertains me to think that you still believe there are ties between us. Between us, to the contrary, there is only a grave. And yet, even so, I would like you to believe that at the bottom of a heart more or less broken, or at any rate chipped, by my inadvertence in not marrying you, I have remained, to a reasonable degree, what, in a general way of speaking, a tolerably indulgent person (after making the proper allowance for man's frailty and the meddlesomeness of other women) might describe as virtually faithful now and then to your memory, in at least a broad-minded and urbane interpretation of that phrase, so far as it goes, and with (as

243

the stock brokers who handle my millions always say in their incomprehensible monthly reports) errors and omissions excepted.

Yes, as a life-long romantic, I would like you to believe something of this sort. But you were not ever, not even in youth, not even in my bed, a fool. You know perfectly that I think you in your present rôle a nuisance. So I may as well admit plainly that I will inscribe the book in my own handwriting because of your handwriting.

＊　　　＊

＊

I did not recognize your writing when I opened your letter along with five other letters; but when I came to read it, in its due season, because I find the process more methodical, somehow, to read first the letters which come in long envelopes, then your letter gave me (after, to be sure, I had looked at the signature) quite an agreeably romantic turn. I remembered, you see, so very many other letters in that same handwriting, and what these letters had once meant to me, a regrettably great while ago.

I remembered our youth and our love and our intense if brief happiness, and I remembered also those heresies in the way of syntax and spelling which once lent to this handwriting an ever-present spice of some slight surprise. I remembered, in short, my extreme devotion to that girl whom time has transformed and amplified into the decisive matron who is now pestering me for an autograph—to adorn the book which is being forwarded "under a separate cover." (That phrase alone rings untrue, let me remark: once it was always "seperate," as I, perhaps alone, have been at unthrifty pains to remember for a good thirty years.) And it seemed, I repeat, an odd thing that no trace of this girl should remain anywhere to-day except in your writing, here on my desk, and in my writing yonder on the bookshelf.

Such was the reflection which turned my thoughts from over-many romantic half-regrets and pensive half-wishes into exercises rather less lofty: for it now occurred to me that, in the outcome, I had utilized you and our ancient love-affair, and all our far-away young joy and heartbreak, after a fashion familiar to every artist in words. Almost all of it was neatly set down somewhere in a neatly printed book with my name on the backbone. Virtually everything I remembered about you was thus preserved (for a little while, anyhow) in some one or another of my numerous writings, so that in my writing also survives the dear girl whom you no longer resemble.

I would much like to assert that (in the definitive edition of my collected works, to be had at all book dealers) she survives forever young and lovely and unchanged, because of my adoring labors, but the truth is not quite that. Twice in those printed pages I discover you in a form fairly recognizable. But for the most part, madam, your relics are uncivilly scattered. Here, I mean, is a phrase, and there a fine inconsistency, which once graced your conversation; in another volume I observe some passages from your letters; and in yet another volume I detect an incident in which you and I figured pleasingly, just as yonder, a great many pages distant, I light upon your nose, and in still another place I find your hair.

Most of that which you once meant to me seems to have been thus broken up, into atoms, as it were; and then redistributed; reblended with my quite other memories of quite other young women; and recolored, no doubt: but all appears to have been used, after a strangely business-like fashion, in the construction of my books; all turned into a staple commodity and sold on a royalty basis for the support of my wife and child. For the true Economist, madam, will waste not even a mistake or an aberration, so that if he but lives long enough, every one of his love-affairs gets into print after considerable beneficent editing.

From these sad and sordid reflections I strayed inevitably into a sort of census-taking of the other women more or less mirrored in my publishings. It was odd to see how many and how various young women had been utilized in this way, as the raw material of my writing. I appeared to have been trifled with by no comely feminine person who did not develop by-and-by, at times wholly, and at other times in the disintegrated fashion of which I have told, into something to write about. Some girls, I decided, had got into my books as individuals, where others survived as mere mincemeat. It followed that no matter how well or how badly each of them had treated me, each had come in the end to the same residuum, in a paragraph or so of very lovingly repolished prose, sold over shop counters for the proper support of my wife and child, and to keep me in cigarettes.

*   *

*

The poet is proverbially unlucky in love. His luck here indeed is super-excellent. Time and again he is jilted, rather as a matter of course, if but because woman, as a practical creature, does not marry a poet so long as more stable helpmates come a-wooing; and it is singular to reflect how many literary masterpieces have resulted from feminine common-sense as displayed on this particular point. No other being lives with quite the gusto of a recently jilted romantic; he is everywhere a-tingle with sensibility: and the superabundance of his woe, of his astonishment, and of his sarcasm, overflows at once into rhetorical expression.

So it has always been, men say, since the first dawn of polite letters, wherein Archilochus of Paros, when thus treated, constructed such a thumping masterpiece out of his lacerated feelings that the false one and all her eight sisters straightway hanged themselves. In this way they made Archilochus famous forever, as the founder of satire, says his legend, which possibly reflects credit on the imagination of his publishers. Nor have I any least doubt that Simonides of Amorgos had but recently been jilted when he likewise established an enduring literary reputation, a bit later, with his fine poem upon the nine sorts of women, who severally (if I may quote this slanderer, madam) resemble swine, and foxes, and bitches, and mud, and asses, and sea-water, and weasels, and mares, and monkeys. To a fond and favored lover no one of these special comparisons, I submit, would occur as inevitable.

So it was, upon varying levels, when Catullus

reviled his Clodia, and Villon his *faulse beaulté*, and Shakespeare his dark wanton, and Pope his Mary Montagu, and Dickens his Maria Beadnell, and when yet hundreds of other writers got from a woman's change of mind the impetus for a masterwork. And so for that matter it remains to-day, when there are but few practising male writers who have not made a so-so book out of the events leading up to their latest divorce.

It may be that all artists are thus quickened and made fertile by their love-affairs: the writer, in any case, takes his unchivalrous toll from the smiles and the frowns of his mistress equally. For, now I think of it, she cannot with any kindness stop the rapscallion from writing. Her kindness is but another spur. If to the one side, Swinburne gets *The Triumph of Time* out of Miss Faulkner's refusal to have anything to do with him, yet in the same milieu does Rossetti derive *The House of Life* from Miss Siddal's fond surrender, and later digs up her corpse so that he may put into immortal print his more lively recollections of her behavior in bed. It follows that a woman has really no say in the outcome: it follows that when once the elect writer has cast her-ward his handkerchief, she may decide whether or not to contribute to his carnal pleasures, but willy-nilly she will contribute to his forthcoming books without stint. And either way, during the delightful toil of eternalizing the supreme passion of his life, in exactly the right words, the man will come to forget all about her.

Well, and just so, I confess, I had put you out of mind with some thoroughness, madam, until I came to read what, at divers times and desks, I had written about you in my collected fictions; and I thus passed naturally to what yet other women had, as we say, inspired me to write. I faced then a discomfort and a quandary common to most romanticists who live to be middle aged.

*   *

*

Instinctively, it would seem, the creative writer will use one young woman after another, in the first place, to heighten his sensibilities. He is so made that from each love-affair, whether his love be requited or rejected, he derives renewed literary vigor; and in this mildly vampirish fashion the beginning writer stays dependent upon women for his continued life as a producer of books. He is so made, in brief, that his sexual excitation will cause him to write (and to write more fluently and more forcibly), not of necessity about his mistress' eyebrows, but as to whatsoever topic he has in hand. I can detect no logic in this sequence, but I know it to be unvarying. I would phrase it that a writer—led, I repeat, by some blind instinct—unlocks a door to release his talents, using one or another young woman as the key. That key need not, let us say, be made of eighteen carat gold; it has served its one purpose, in at least any literary connection, when once the door is unclosed; and that key is in no manner allied with what later comes through the doorway.

Meanwhile the creative writer observes, and makes mental notes as to, his enforced collaborator, in a fashion rather more microscopic than it is chivalrous. In the moment that he adores most hotly, he will be dissecting austerely. His thoughts will anatomize in some sort both himself and the recumbent female whom his arms happen to be embracing, in the while that his tongue babbles ecstasy. He amasses, in brief, an inestimable collection of memories; and upon these he gets to work, in due season, as his raw material.

Thereafter he will re-create the women whom he has loved, and he sets them a-moving in his books. He improves them jealously, beyond human recognition, until they have become in their every endowment worthy to be loved, or to be execrated, with the full force of his vocabulary. And he delights in them consumedly, these women who are his own amended and corrected versions of nature's mediocre output.

He comes, too, to put faith in them. Memory is the best of all editors, provided always you like a high-hearted romance. Memory is very adroit to soften hazily all harshness, to enhance some spirited doing with a yet bolder outline, to recolor advantageously, to abridge the unsatisfying, and to insert here and there a neatly restrained touch of heroism, whensover any man considers his past. Like all fine artists, memory is also a skilled plagiarist, taking unostentatiously, with an assured hand, its own whencesoever it offers. So does it come about that since every creative writer invents for himself a superior past, peopled for the most part with goddesses, the man's memory adopts it admiringly, quietly, unalterably, as his actual past for all working purposes.

The peripeteia hereabouts is in fact rather droll. The creative writer in his day dreams touches up, through mere force of habit, this or the other happening and makes of it that which, in circumstances a bit altered, might have occurred somewhat more satisfyingly in his life: then by-and-by the unconscionable plagiarist, memory, reassures him that the affair did happen thus and not otherwise. And he, the eternal child, attends to this glib romancing with a child's delight, much pleased and all credulous, accepting as pure gold a false coinage of his own minting.

Most eloquent and particularly convincing is that so illimitably gifted liar, called memory, as to the girls whom the attendant romantic once knew. That which he has written about them, he is persuaded, survives but as pale travesty and inept understatement. These girls were not as are

the run of young females: he has trafficked, it
seems to him, with sylphs, and hamadryads, and
succubæ, and angels, and vampires, and sala-
manders, and saints, and ghouls, and troll
maidens, and loreleis, and with yet other divine
fair ones of all mythologic degrees, transcendent
variously in their innocence or their amatory in-
ventions or their faithlessness.

Earth at all events knows no longer such loveliness as in his day was plentiful as blackberries.
He regards the young, the uncurved, the with-
out-waist, the flat-bosomed, the hipless, the un-
haunched, the not-ever-tranquil females of an
inferior genus, *Homo*, as these sprightly mam-
mals flutter and chatter everywhither; and he
wonders through what aberration the pursuing
boy can believe this brisk, meagre creature to be
a girl? It is not even shaped like a girl; it is upon
the whole more fashioned after the shaping of
an eel, or of a lank dragon-fly unwinged, or of
an animated broomstraw: and he reflects sadly
upon the lean pasturage which a discerning
young man must find nowanights in unlicensed
beds.

But thirty years ago—then there were goddesses. All earth was populous with divine girlhood. And its dear possessors came to you unworthy; they came one by one, as philanthropists, ungirdled, yielding without parsimony an opulence of well curved and fair colored charms; they came, in those remote times, as fondly as Venus came to Anchises, as alertly as Diana might approach an Endymion who had no least present thoughts of sleeping, or as daintily as Titania came to Nick Bottom. *Eheu, fugaces!* remarks the creative writer inevitably, if but he happens to be a profound classical scholar.

*　　　*

*

Meanwhile another reviser is at work on precisely the same raw material. As the creative writer transforms in print, and in memory also, the most dear or the most heartless girls whom his youth knew, and got a heart-stirring profit of, so does time no less zealously transform them in fact. From the bright eyes time saps the brightness, about them etching wrinkles, beneath each of them producing a bagginess, either brownly speckled, like two guinea eggs, or of a crinkly putrescent blue. Soft cheeks he turns weather-beaten, and into all lustrous hair he weaves dull cobwebs, in the while that under his skilled touch the curved lips sag, teeth loosen, and additional chins develop. In yet other quarters of the feminine body does time reorder matters, very much as time did for La Belle Heaulmière; we need not go into all that quite as explicitly as Villon did; but I agree perforce with Villon that the result is dreadful.

It is particularly dreadful, though, for the appalled romanticist who has thrice idealized these women, in youth and in his books and in fond recollections, when he encounters these flesh-and-blood parodies of his deceased loves. He can in fact but question his own sanity whensoever he attempts to think of anybody (even their own luckless husbands) who could so madly intermingle temerity and ill taste as to address these repulsive if wholly respectable matrons amorously. And is it possible, he marvels, that they were always so dull-witted? or was it somebody else who in youth was an idiot? and how too could quite so many of them upon their wedding nights prevent the bridegroom from a discovery hurtful to his pride? All these questions an aging poet revolves forlornly: and I think that the women who provoke such perturbations ought in mere mercy to keep away from the poor man.

But they do not. They to the contrary will ask him (in the most unwarrantable fashion, madam) to autograph the very books which he has made out of his traffic with them. They will cackle. They will speak witlessly. I have known them to belch. They are capable, I stammer to relate it, they are capable of nudging their erstwhile adorer, with a large and leering informality, such as Dante would not have put up with for one moment in Beatrice, such as Samson would hardly have endured from Delilah. Upon yet more dreadful occasions they become coy. They seem, in fact, to be but inadequately impressed by the talents which they were once privileged to nourish: and at times they regard the present-day owner of these talents with a certain dark significance, as of one knowing derogatory secrets about him which he himself does not know.

About Loveliness Revised

It follows, madam, that I detest and avoid all such women. And yet I wonder, too, that so much of loyalty and of happiness, and of our youth's fine magnanimity, should now lie buried, so very deep, in that grave across which we face each other.

*   *

*

THE EPISTLE
EGOTISTIC

*

*   *

"Rich man, poor man, beggar man, thief,
Doctor, lawyer, Indian chief."

THE EPISTLE EGOTISTIC

*　　*

*

*C*hrough *what mania, friend, need you deliver*
to the world these familiar letters? But yesterday
did you oppress us with much year-long prattle
as to your uneventful doings, your pointless
whims, and with your tiny thoughts, of how
slight marrow and how slender ambitiousness!
Now that you reply to sundry fools who pester
you without any malice, and who are led into
molestation by no prompter save their own folly,
now yet again must you bid the large world
listen to your petty frets, and heed a fool speaking to his own peers with petulance. Not thus
does the philosopher endure small ills.

Moreover you speak without enough reticence
your actual thinking, and have not garnished it
with grave magnanimities. That is not well. It is
meet that in a world ruled by the dull-minded

a writer should be dull decorously, and so win for himself respectful applause. It is wise that the maker of essays should concern himself with altruism and with great modern trends of thought and with the future of humanity and with yet other ponderable matters. Let him bear in mind that his views upon communism, when once they have been made judiciously incomprehensible, can be inserted with marked advantage almost anywhere. Nor will prophesying, provided only that it involve not less than four nations in a destruction sufficiently gory, at any time be found amiss. Let him assert, too, that we live nowadays in a changing world: it is an abstruse reflection which the young have received favorably since the prime of Heraclitus.

Let the wise maker of essays speak, in brief, with an assured conviction, as to that which has weightiness, hiding his large ignorance of his own import with large words, and instructing his hearers high-mindedly in all departments of the immense. Let him don dignity, and whinny with due solemnness, whensoever he prints. A very many will hearken to his *ducdame*: the publishers of that maker of essays will call him blessed.

*   *

*

But you, friend, fare alone, perceiving too curiously the folly of your fellows and of your own doings. You forget that you also might be a seer and a martyr in your own estimation, and so be unlifted hugeously, did you not abstain from this one foolishness only. You should accredit yourself with more profound thoughts: if they be nonsense, how few will detect it! Nor will many persons heed this detection, in a world for the most part populated, and in its every part controlled, by the dull-minded.

I counsel you to desist from speaking truthfully about those little matters which continue in your daily thoughts to amuse you, and which keep mirthful your quiet living. When the dull-minded pester you with irrational letters you do well to smile at the folly of these letters. Yet, ah, infatuate! when you summon any other persons to smile with you, then has your doing a more doubtful reward. The dull are many in numbers: they do not smile at the deeds of one another: him that smiles at any time-hallowed dullness they regard as a frivolous fellow, as a piddler with vain notions, and as a witless trifler; for all dullness is found acceptable in the eyes of the dull.

But you fare alone, compromising with the dull-minded unvaliantly in your utterances, indeed, yet offending them through your gestures unprofitably. You shrug too often, without any frank or well-thought-of reason. You avoid the immense a little timorously. Into the drift of new days you forbear to pry after dreams as large and ardent as those which swayed your far-away youth-time. Then you had grief, love, and laughter: now you are merely smug, and a life neither tragic nor blissful you think a desirable traffic. All that is done, you protest, seems well done with; your playthings content you; all that impends must be met, God willing, without any whining. So much alone you have gained from the half of a century's schooling—platitudes flavored with gratitude. Such is life's stinted

tuition's end, in so far as you fathom it. That,
and that only, you tell us.

*   *

*

To what readers, friend, may you despatch with
any confidence this little book of familiar letters? It does not teach: it foretells no cataclysms:
it does not inspire self-righteousness. It may look
to find no lover among those persons whom the
ancient rhyme lists.

What care has the rich man, or the poor man
either, to be told of those thin subtleties which
you have set down in these same letters as to
your religion and concerning your art? May the
beggar man pause in his alms-asking, or the thief
avert from well-paying larcenies, to attend your
talking about a mirror and pigeons? What is it
to the doctor that a child asks for your autograph, or that yet another young loon plans to
become a writer? When such tidings arrive, the
doctor can but shrug and return to his *Medical
Journal*.

Special Delivery

Nay, and will the lawyer put away his torts, and forget affidavits, when you tell him that many books are written by dullards, and are reviewed handsomely by dullards, or that yet other dullards collect these books without ever reading them? Upon what reservation is it strange news to the Indian chief that a young squaw may desire to be rid of her maidenhead, or that in serene middle life a Christian gentlewoman may wear two chins, or it may be three chins, disadvantageously? Here is much cry and but little wool: you speak of things known to Agamemnon. In Babylon were such matters familiar. It may well be that in his mother's arms Cain also heard his parents talking about these truisms.

Yet do these tiny and trite comedies amuse you as though they were performed for the first time. You find in small human follies an unfailing zest. When the inane pester you, then do you play at anger unavailingly: your brows frown, but beneath them your lips are smiling at the droll ways of men and women; your vanity also is tickled when you perceive that anybody, even such blockheads, can regard you seriously.

The Epistle Egotistic

Did the postman approach you empty-handed upon any morning, you who revile his advent would abate in complacency. You would be stricken with perturbed dismay. Who doubts that when the children of Israel had passed safely through the Red Sea, who doubts that afterward the surviving Egyptians found life to be a rather flat business when bereft of its daily plague? *Odi et amo*, quoth Catullus, of the woman whom he detested and yet loved. Well, and about your unsought correspondents you may truthfully say the same thing.

EXPLICIT

BIBLIOGRAPHICAL

* *

*

Some portion of this little book has been honored, during 1932-33, by a scattered and partial printing in the pages of perhaps over-partial magazines. It follows that to each of these magazines I desire in this place to extend due thanks for all wayside hospitalities.

And I itemize, in so far as at this writing proves possible:—

(a) In *The Bookman* were published, very much as they hereinbefore figure, the first, the second, the third, the eighth, and the tenth letter.

(b) Two extracts from the fourth letter appeared in *The American Spectator*, wherein these fragments were entitled severally "Study in Sincerity" and "Prose of a Pallbearer."

(c) Much of the sixth letter made its typographic début in the guise of a preface to Mr. I. R.

Brussel's *Bibliography of James Branch Cabell*, yet another section of this letter being printed, in the first issue of *The American Spectator*, as "The Genteel Tradition in Sex."

(d) The fifth letter was apportioned, after the same economical fashion, between *The Saturday Review of Literature* (wherein a great deal of this letter appeared under its present title) and *The American Spectator*, which last-named periodical presented its own chosen extract under the at best equivocal heading, "Commonplaces."

*9 7 8 0 8 0 9 5 3 3 5 3 4 *